GETTING PUBLICITY

Tana Fletcher
Julia Rockler

Self-Counsel Press
(*a division of*)
International Self-Counsel Press Ltd.
Canada   USA

Self-Counsel Press acknowledges the financial support of the Government of Canada through the Book Publishing Industry Development Program (BPID) for our publishing activities.

Printed in Canada.

First edition: 1990; Reprinted: 1991
Second edition: 1995
Third edition: 2000

Canadian Cataloguing in Publication Data

Fletcher, Tana.
    Getting publicity

    (Self-counsel business series)
    ISBN 1-55180-312-7

    1. Publicity. I. Rockler, Julia. II. Title. III. Series.
HM1226.F43 2000   659   C00-910572-7

Self-Counsel Press
(*a division of*)
International Self-Counsel Press Ltd.

1481 Charlotte Road	1704 N. State Street
North Vancouver, BC V7J 1H1	Bellingham, WA 98225
Canada	USA

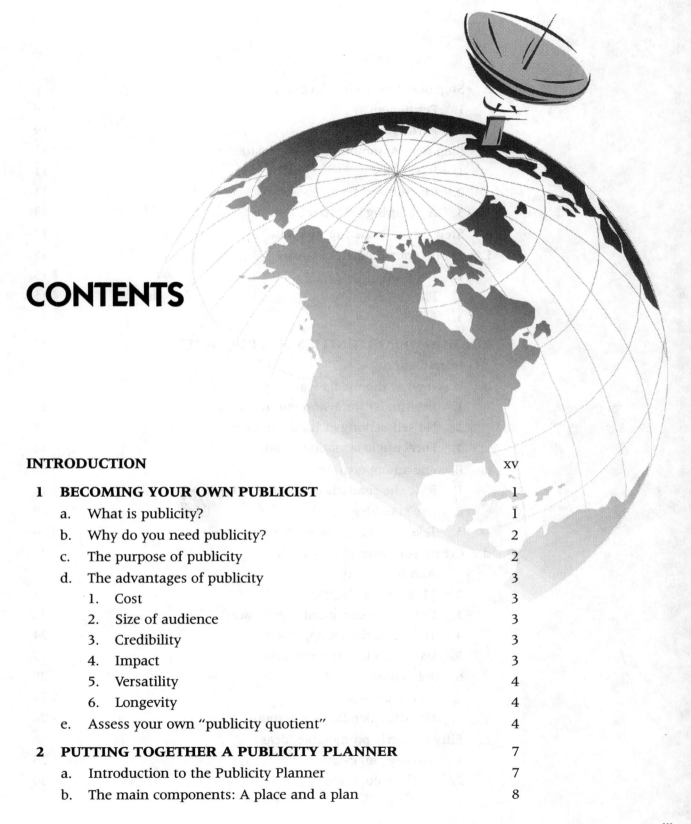

CONTENTS

WORKSHEETS

SAMPLES

CHECKLISTS

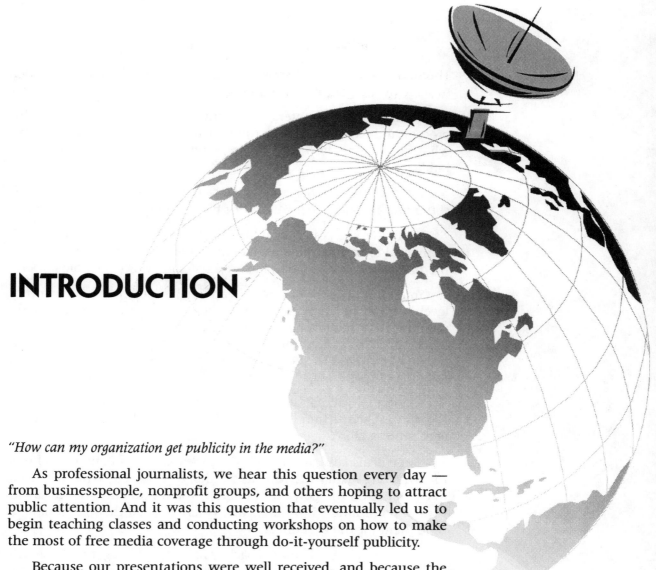

INTRODUCTION

"How can my organization get publicity in the media?"

As professional journalists, we hear this question every day — from businesspeople, nonprofit groups, and others hoping to attract public attention. And it was this question that eventually led us to begin teaching classes and conducting workshops on how to make the most of free media coverage through do-it-yourself publicity.

Because our presentations were well received, and because the demand for our classes began to increase, we decided to put all of our "inside" information down on paper and create this book — a combination instructional manual and reference guide — for business owners, entrepreneurs, and publicity-seekers everywhere.

Our goal in this project was simple: to demonstrate that anyone can learn the skills necessary to profit from free publicity. Regardless of an individual's business, budget, or background, with the proper knowledge and the right tools, anyone can become a media magnet.

The chapters in this book are arranged to help you direct your efforts in an organized manner. In the first chapter, you'll find a short quiz for rating your personal "Publicity Quotient" before you proceed.

Then, in chapter 2, we'll show you how to set up a Publicity Planner to serve as the permanent basis for your entire publicity program.

In subsequent chapters, we'll guide you through the publicity process and explain the four fundamental components of publicity: what to publicize, how to publicize, where to publicize, and when to publicize.

You'll learn which activities attract the most attention, how to communicate with the media, and when to build on previous publicity.

We'll give you pointers on targeting the various types of media — from local to national to international, and from print to broadcast to the Internet — with an emphasis on reaching every possible outlet.

You'll discover the secrets of capitalizing on the media at every level — from the smallest neighborhood newsletters through trade and industrial publications to the largest television networks and the World Wide Web. In addition, we'll address a number of advanced publicity techniques, such as conducting press conferences, making public service announcements, and using video news releases.

Along the way, you'll learn how to make use of all of the tools of the self-publicist's trade — from writing news releases to putting together press kits.

You will also discover hundreds of inexpensive and practical hints for attracting media attention as we show you exactly what you need to capitalize on the power of publicity. You'll find out what to say in your announcements to the media, where to send them, and how to time them for the best effect.

As a bonus, we'll even coach you on preparing for those all-important media interviews, with advice on rehearsing your answers, choosing your wardrobe, and applying your makeup.

By the final chapter, you'll be eager to launch your own well-planned publicity campaign, confident in the knowledge that you possess the skills necessary to succeed. Throughout the text, worksheets and checklists will aid you in setting your priorities and achieving your objectives. Sample publicity material will provide you with easy-to-follow examples. And professional tips will add polish to all of your efforts. No matter what your purpose, if you are interested in pursuing publicity, you will find the help you need right here.

During the past several years we have helped many people put themselves in the media spotlight. Now we want to help you.

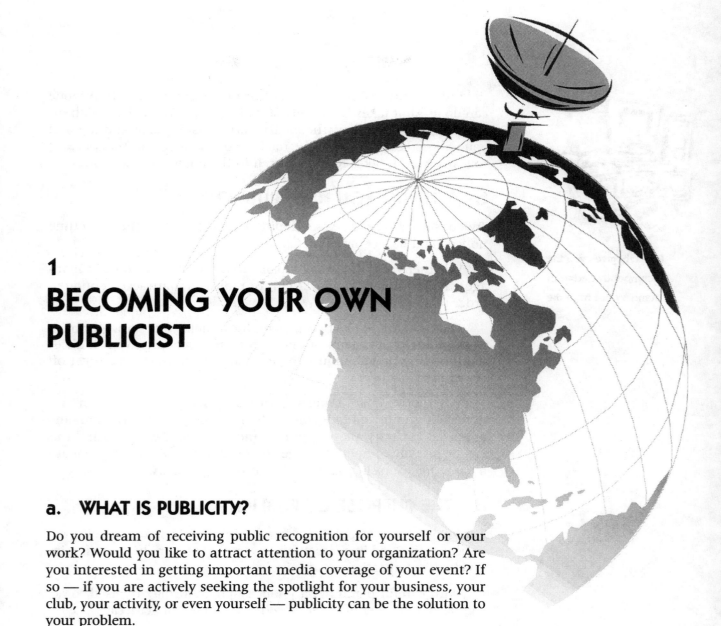

1
BECOMING YOUR OWN PUBLICIST

a. WHAT IS PUBLICITY?

Do you dream of receiving public recognition for yourself or your work? Would you like to attract attention to your organization? Are you interested in getting important media coverage of your event? If so — if you are actively seeking the spotlight for your business, your club, your activity, or even yourself — publicity can be the solution to your problem.

And just what is publicity? Publicity is what you use to get attention without paying for it. Publicity is the key to letting people know what you do.

The most usual source of publicity is the media — that is, any public communications medium from a newsletter to network television and cybercommunications, although something as simple as word of mouth can be a source of publicity too.

Publicity is what you use to get attention without paying for it.

1

Publicity gives you the competitive edge of standing out from the crowd.

It doesn't take a rare talent to learn how to get publicity. Anyone can do it. All it takes is an understanding of the rules, along with inside information on how the media work. Master the procedures and you will make the most of the media. So grab a pencil. You're about to learn what it takes to put yourself in the publicity limelight.

b. WHY DO YOU NEED PUBLICITY?

Two obstacles face everyone hoping to succeed in business: getting noticed and producing profits.

Whether you run a small repair service from your home or manage an international organization, you must first attract attention in order to prosper.

That's where publicity comes in. It can help you boost your business, promote your nonprofit group, or simply enhance your individual image by providing just the lift your enterprise needs to get off the ground.

Whether you're offering a service, selling a product, or running a nonprofit group, you face competition for the public's attention and approval. Publicity allows you to stand out from the crowd and this can be just the competitive edge you need. If you are hoping to make a name for yourself, you need the power of publicity.

c. THE PURPOSE OF PUBLICITY

The major goals of publicity are to stimulate business activity, enhance profits, and increase public awareness of a product, service, individual, organization, or activity.

With careful planning, a publicity program may be used to accomplish a number of other objectives as well. Publicity can —

- ◆ magnify visibility
- ◆ create intense interest in a one-time event
- ◆ be part of an ongoing promotion
- ◆ turn a hobby into a business
- ◆ help you to get a head start on the competition
- ◆ establish a new image to replace an outdated one
- ◆ aid in breaking out of a sales slump

- get a new venture off the ground
- provide a test market for a new idea
- generate good will

d. THE ADVANTAGES OF PUBLICITY

Publicity offers six main advantages over other types of promotional tools.

1. Cost

Advertising and publicity both make use of the media to reach the public, but publicity is considerably less expensive. In fact, unlike advertising, where companies must pay for time and space in the media, publicity coverage is virtually free. In most cases, the only expenses for publicity are for paper and postage to mail announcements to the media.

2. Size of audience

Publicity is powerful. It can tell your story to thousands of potential customers — maybe even millions if you use the mass media. While you would probably benefit by taking your message individually to persons who might be interested, it is much faster and more effective to reach the public in great numbers.

3. Credibility

Publicity lends an air of credibility that's missing in advertising. When you are interviewed on the six o'clock news or quoted in the daily paper, the public tends to perceive you as an expert. Media attention is usually viewed by listeners and viewers as a de facto endorsement of your product, service, or cause.

4. Impact

Publicity is persuasive. It can shape public opinion, mold personal images, and even reverse negative attitudes. Book publishers, for example, send free copies of their books to critics in the hope that reviews will provide positive publicity for authors. Movie stars appear on television talk shows to publicize their latest cinematic efforts. And corporate executives hold press conferences to tell their side of the story in ecological controversies.

Before becoming your own publicist, assess your "Publicity Quotient" — your knowledge of publicity procedures and practices.

5. Versatility

Publicity can be used to place you in the spotlight at almost any time and in any place you choose. By availing yourself of carefully selected media opportunities, you can expand into new markets or even launch a brand new business.

6. Longevity

Publicity offers longevity by providing you with a permanent record. Once you have been mentioned in the media, you can show the clipping to potential clients, quote it in your advertising, or use it as a means to garner more publicity.

e. ASSESS YOUR OWN "PUBLICITY QUOTIENT"

At least once in your life you have probably met a business owner who has relied on "word of mouth" to bring in new customers. But when you know how to capitalize on publicity, and you have your plan in place, you won't need to wait for such uncertain referrals. By becoming your own publicist and practicing the art of self-promotion, *you* possess the power to start people talking.

So why wait? Start today and soon you'll be prepared to overcome obscurity and make a name for yourself in the media.

You first need to assess your "Publicity Quotient." You may be surprised at what you already know — and what you don't know. Turn to Worksheet 1 to test your knowledge. Answers and instructions for rating yourself follow.

WORKSHEET 1
TEST YOUR P.Q.*

Answer true or false to the following questions. Then see below for the answers and how to score yourself.

1. It is necessary to "know someone" in the press to receive free publicity.   True or False _____

2. Sending invitations to the media is a waste of time because nobody ever responds to them.   True or False _____

3. Advertisers are offered free publicity according to the amount of money they spend on commercials.   True or False _____

4. Only spokespersons for big corporations and major industries are qualified to appear on radio and television talk shows.   True or False _____

5. Threatening to discontinue your advertising is an effective way to make the media pay attention to you.   True or False _____

6. It is more profitable to promote a special, one-time event than to pursue publicity for routine activities.   True or False _____

7. Contributing to a charitable cause is good publicity.   True or False _____

8. Sending gifts or offering to buy meals for reporters is an accepted way to get coverage of an event.   True or False _____

9. Members of the media appreciate your calling them whenever you think of a possible story idea.   True or False _____

10. Publicity efforts are wasted unless they appear in influential publications or on important television programs.   True or False _____

11. Creating a Web page is the best way to reach people on the Internet.   True or False _____

ANSWERS TO THE P.Q. QUIZ

1. False. These days you don't need to "know someone" at the local paper or have a relative who works on a television show to get your name in the news. There are simply too many pages and too many hours to fill for journalists to feature only their friends. The truth is, the media needs you at least as much as you need them.

2. False. Every piece of mail received by the media will be read — or at least glanced at. The trick is knowing how to package your presentation professionally for maximum impact.

3. False. Publicity is not doled out to big spenders. In order to prosper, the media needs to attract readers and viewers through interesting stories, not by paying back favors.

*Publicity Quotient: Your knowledge of publicity practices and procedures.

4. False. Well-informed individuals in every field are welcomed by broadcasters. In fact, once you learn the secrets, you can actually become a sought-after media celebrity.

5. False. Reporters have no idea how much you spend on advertising and don't care. More important, they resent being told what to do by outsiders.

6. False. It's more effective to plan an ongoing publicity program and have your name appear in print every week than to create a big splash and then disappear without a ripple. A well-organized publicity campaign makes even routine activities sound interesting.

7. False. Participating in a charitable event — or in any event, for that matter — is not publicity at all unless others hear about it. Learning to blow your own horn, to proclaim your accomplishments in public, is what publicity is all about.

8. False. Payola might get you coverage, all right, but probably not the type you want. Good journalists never expect to leave an assignment with anything but a story.

9. False. Avoid telephoning members of the media unless it is an emergency. Journalists love to learn about suitable story ideas, but prefer to receive them through the mail.

10. False. Publicity is never a waste as long as you know how to take full advantage of it. Through time-proven techniques, you can learn to parlay a tiny article in a suburban shopper into a feature story on national television.

11. False. It's not enough to create a Web page, unless you have a way to attract visitors to see it. You'll need to hone your skills at Internet outreach.

SCORING YOUR PUBLICITY QUOTIENT

9 to 11: On the brink of media success
You have a thorough understanding of how the media works and what the rules are. You are ready to learn how to plan a publicity campaign that will get attention.

7 or 8: Somewhat savvy
Although you have some sense of how publicity works, you aren't completely clear about the role of the media. Once you learn more about the machinery, you'll know how to press the right buttons.

5 or 6: A few lessons are in order
You haven't yet mastered the media. You'll find it much easier to navigate your way through the media maze once you have a good map.

3 or 4: Neophyte
You may have had some exposure to reporters, but you are lacking "inside" knowledge. You need to study the basics before embarking on a publicity program.

2 or below: No time to lose
You are missing out on some wonderful opportunities to promote your business because you don't know how to attract media attention. Learn the rules, however, and you can win the publicity game.

2
PUTTING TOGETHER A PUBLICITY PLANNER

a. INTRODUCTION TO THE PUBLICITY PLANNER

Can you imagine attempting to build a skyscraper without blueprints or trying to drive through Europe without a map? Of course not. In order to achieve anything worthwhile, you need a clear vision of where you're headed.

In the same way, publicity deserves a plan — a diagram of where you're going and a schedule showing when you will arrive. Before you actually implement a publicity program, therefore, you will need to set up a Publicity Planner. This sounds impressive, but it is simply a place to store your materials and a system for setting down your strategies.

If publicity is to be effective, it must be a continuous process — an ongoing program aimed at getting your name before the public and *keeping* it there. Therefore, before you start to publicize yourself,

Your Publicity Planner will become the center of your publicity-related activities, so put in the effort to make it outstanding!

you should have worked out not only how to pursue publicity regularly, but also how you are going to respond to the attention you receive and build on the interest you generate.

For that reason you will benefit by taking time now to set up a permanent Publicity Planner. This will be the basis of your entire publicity program. It will, in fact, become the "publicity department" of your organization.

Once your Publicity Planner is in place it will become the center of your publicity-related activities. It will enable you to keep track of all the elements of your publicity campaign from the earliest planning stages through the actual implementation of your campaign. With this type of organized system, you'll always be prepared to act as well as to react.

In this chapter you will find out what you need to create your own personalized Publicity Planner. In addition to instructions for choosing a spot and setting up your files, you will find a shopping list for all the basic necessities. In each subsequent chapter, you will learn a little more about what to store in your Publicity Planner — media correspondence, publicity photographs, mailing lists, and other materials — along with recommendations about buying additional items.

By the end of the book, your Publicity Planner will be complete and you'll be ready to embark on your first campaign.

You can get a head start right now by purchasing your first item: a notebook to keep by your side at all times as you read this book. That way you'll be ready to write down your shopping list of supplies along with any ideas you have about planning your own personalized publicity.

b. THE MAIN COMPONENTS: A PLACE AND A PLAN

Your Publicity Planner will have two main components: a place and a plan. "Place" refers to the physical location you set aside for the filing system which is the basis of the Publicity Planner. And "plan" means your blueprint for action — your schedule for sending announcements and conducting promotional events.

Truly effective media promotion will result only when you are in control of both elements, place and plan, because successful publicity is like sound construction: a sturdy structure needs a solid foundation. Whether you are a self-employed consultant looking for new clients in your own neighborhood or the marketing manager for a multinational conglomerate, the results you achieve depend on how much care you take in laying your groundwork.

c. STEP ONE: CHOOSING A LOCATION

Once you decide to pursue publicity on a regular basis, designate a specific area for your Publicity Planner. As you read through the following sections, visualize yourself going through the motions — sending announcements to the media, responding to telephone calls from the press, and scheduling promotional activities. Then think about the location that would be most convenient for you. That way, when you are ready to purchase your supplies and set up your system, you will know just where to put everything.

Because the Publicity Planner is actually nothing more than a filing system for keeping track of paperwork such as press clippings, typed announcements, media lists, and publicity photographs, the physical space required is approximately equivalent to the area needed for storing 25 or 30 file folders.

And no matter how large — or small — your Publicity Planner or how frequently you use it, it nevertheless deserves a designated location. You can use the corner of your desk, one shelf of your bookcase, or a single drawer in your file cabinet, but whichever location you select, storing all of your materials together will save time and energy.

It pays to give serious consideration to setting up your Publicity Planner, because beginning on a solid basis is one way to give your publicity attempts that extra edge over the competition. But keep in mind that, when aiming for a smooth-running program, only you can decide which system will work best for your own situation.

One of the biggest "start-up" decisions you will have to make, for example, is to choose between the two basic equipment options: permanent and portable. Both alternatives have merit, but in order to select wisely you should understand the differences between the two.

1. Permanent

Assigning a permanent spot for your Publicity Planner, such as one drawer in your office filing cabinet, provides stability to your program. By placing publicity next to payroll, inventory, and other information

Should your Publicity Planner be permenant or portable? It all depends on your situation.

that is important to your business, you ascribe a permanence to it and acknowledge it as an essential element in your enterprise.

Additionally, a permanent spot makes the Publicity Planner easily accessible, not only to you, but to everyone else who might need it. In an emergency, anyone can find the necessary information readily.

If you decide to establish a permanent location, then you might simply opt to purchase new file folders for your existing file system. In the beginning, plan to dedicate at least 25 folders to your Publicity Planner. And make sure you have enough space in your file cabinet or drawer for adding more Publicity Planner files.

2. Portable

In many cases, portability may be more valuable than permanence. In a nonprofit organization, for instance, where the individual in charge of publicity often changes from year to year, a portable system might make the transition easier. And when the publicity work is done from a member's home, a portable system is especially beneficial, allowing for convenient transportation of records.

Business owners who occasionally work at home also appreciate the advantage of easily movable files, as do those home-based entrepreneurs whose "office" rotates regularly from the kitchen table to the spare bedroom.

If you think you would prefer to work with a portable system, then you have a number of styles from which to choose, all available through office supply stores and catalogues.

The simplest filing system is a plastic or metal free-standing rack, with slots designed to hold ten or twelve manila folders in an upright position. With four tiny, rubber-footed legs, this system can be placed on a desktop, a bookshelf, or a table.

Another transportable system is the plastic cube that holds hanging files. Some brands are even designed to be stacked, an advantage when you need to expand your Publicity Planner.

And, finally, there is the suitcase-style file box, usually fashioned from metal or molded plastic, with a carrying handle. Because it closes securely, this option is especially valuable out-of-doors as a protection against damage from rain and snow.

d. STEP TWO: ASSEMBLING THE NECESSITIES

Most of the materials in the self-publicist's tool kit are actually basic office supplies. It is helpful to organize all of the necessary items in advance in order to save time once you are involved in generating media coverage.

Once you have decided whether you want a permanent or a portable Publicity Planner, and where you want to put it, you are ready to purchase —

(a) a filing system (or designate space in your existing system),

(b) at least 25 file folders in the style that fits your filing system, and

(c) the right kind of labels for identifying your file folders.

1. Basic files

Starting now and continuing throughout the book you will be labeling file folders for your Publicity Planner. Although you can customize your own system in any way, every Publicity Planner does include certain basic files, beginning with the following three:

- *Business cards:* It is often a good idea to enclose one of your business cards in your letters to members of the media, so keep a supply handy in your Publicity Planner.

- *Brochures:* If your organization has any printed brochures, store several in a file folder for sending to the media when appropriate.

- *Stationery:* All of your correspondence with the media must be typed on business letterhead stationery. This not only provides the recipients with all the pertinent information they will need, it also helps the media to recognize the legitimacy of your endeavor.

- *Computer files:* All of your computer files relating to publicity should be backed up and kept in your Publicity Planner.

2. Customized files

The Publicity Planner is a flexible file that can be geared to meet the specific needs of any enterprise. All of the various resources and materials that you will eventually choose to store in it will be based on your personal goals and expectations. As you read through the next

Your Publicity Planner should contain industry news, clippings and quotes, promotion ideas, publicity photos, a calendar, and media names, addresses, and correspondence.

chapters and begin to assess your own aspirations, you will be able to pick and choose from a number of different options and gradually set up an individualized program that is perfect for you.

Until that time, however, here's a look ahead at some of the other items you might eventually be storing in your folders, depending on your final plan.

- ◆ *Correspondence:* Whenever you communicate — in writing — with the media, you will need to keep copies filed in chronological order. The most recent correspondence is kept in front of this file; your earliest letter will be at the back.

- ◆ *Industry news:* You'll want to keep on top of the developments in your field in order to have that kind of expertise at your command. As this collection of information grows, you might even need to break it into separate file folders, arranged by categories.

- ◆ *Clippings and quotes:* Every time you are mentioned in the print media, you should "clip" or cut and save the article. Later in the book you will receive specific instructions for making copies of your clippings and using them to generate additional coverage.

- ◆ *Promotion ideas:* To make sure that you don't forget or overlook any publicity possibilities, you should keep all your ideas in one place. As you read through this book, for example, you'll undoubtedly come up with dozens of original concepts. Whenever this happens, write them down and file them for future reference.

- ◆ *Media list:* A list of media names and addresses is probably the single most important element in any Publicity Planner. You'll want to hold off on any purchase of a new address system until you have read chapter 9 section **c. Prepare a Media List,** so that you will be able to choose the style that will work best for you.

- ◆ *Publicity photos:* You'll get instructions for publicity photographs in chapter 6. After you have determined which pictures you plan to use, you'll be able to make extra copies and keep them at hand in your Publicity Planner.

3. A planning calendar

As previously noted, successful publicity requires a plan — a road map detailing where you're going and how you hope to get there. Eventually this plan will be written down and followed when you're engaging in promotional activities and communicating with the media.

Therefore, because nearly all your efforts at promotion will be scheduled in advance, the final item you'll need for your Publicity Planner is a one-year calendar for noting your plans and keeping track of your commitments. For some people a diary or "journal" format is most comfortable, while for others a monthly grid is preferable. When purchasing your personal calendar, just keep in mind that the style doesn't matter as long as it's convenient to use and has room for writing instructions and reminders.

e. STEP THREE: PREPARING THE PLAN

Like your other business goals, publicity requires planning, knowledge, and effort. At the beginning you must ask yourself how much public attention you are seeking. That answer will help determine the amount of time you'll need to devote to your publicity program.

For example, an occasional mention in your community newspaper might take a weekly commitment of an hour or two to plan your campaign and prepare your materials, whereas an interview on national television could require as much as eight or ten hours per week over a period of months. It is up to you to decide how much time you can set aside for publicity tasks and eventually to start marking your calendar accordingly.

At this point, you should begin to consider your personal publicity goals. This means taking a look at several factors, including the audience you hope to reach through your efforts, the amount of media attention you are hoping to generate, and the time you are willing to spend pursuing publicity.

Although your goals will undoubtedly change with time, an initial sense of where you're heading is important if you want to keep your publicity plans on track. To help you envision your goals, turn to Worksheet 2 and answer the questions. Once you have your goals outlined, the next chapter will help you understand what it will take to reach those goals.

WORKSHEET 2
ASSESSING YOUR PUBLICITY GOALS

1. What are your long-range and short-range publicity goals?

   ❑ To announce specific events you are sponsoring

   ❑ To create greater public awareness of your organization's activities

   ❑ To attract new clients or new members

   ❑ To expand your market to include new geographical areas

   ❑ To enhance your personal or organizational image

   ❑ To diversify your business

   ❑ To become a nationally known expert and thereby command higher fees for your services

   ❑ To turn your hobby into your career

   ❑ Other (describe):

   _____

   _____

2. Whom would you like to reach through your publicity?

   ❑ Small sets of localized or specialized customers

   ❑ Large groups of individuals or businesses with a specific interest

   ❑ The general public in a particular community

   ❑ The general public nationwide or even worldwide

   ❑ Other (describe):

   _____

   _____

3. Where do most of your clients or contributors get information about you and your colleagues or competitors?

   ❑ Local newspapers

   ❑ Local radio and television

   ❑ National magazine coverage

❏ National radio and television

❏ Other, including any specialized media (describe):

_____

_____

4. How much time are you planning to devote to your publicity efforts on a regular basis?

a. Daily: Less than one hour ❏

One to two hours ❏

b. Weekly: Less than one hour ❏

One to two hours ❏

Two to four hours ❏

c. Monthly: Less than one hour ❏

One to two hours ❏

Two to four hours ❏

Four to six hours ❏

f. SET UP YOUR PUBLICITY PLANNER

At this point you are ready to begin setting up your Publicity Planner.

1. Location

Designate part of an existing file or buy a new filing system to hold your folders.

2. File folders

To start you'll need approximately 25 file folders.

3. Labels

You can simply write on the tab of your file folders, or you might prefer to type headings on labels. Begin by designating the following folders:

- brochures
- business cards
- clippings and quotes
- correspondence
- industry news
- media list
- promotion ideas
- publicity photographs
- stationery
- computer files
- calendar system

You can choose a one-month grid, a wall display, a day-by-day diary, or whichever calendar style suits you. If you already have a business calendar, make sure it remains with your Publicity Planner. Use it to schedule the actual time you will spend on your publicity-related activities and to jot down any ideas that occur to you about possible promotional activities in the future.

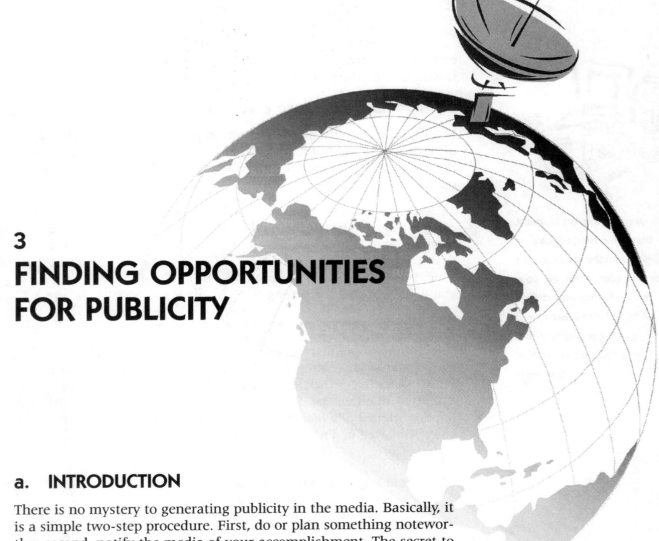

3
FINDING OPPORTUNITIES FOR PUBLICITY

a. INTRODUCTION

There is no mystery to generating publicity in the media. Basically, it is a simple two-step procedure. First, do or plan something noteworthy; second, notify the media of your accomplishment. The secret to success lies in finding activities that not only draw public attention to your enterprise, but also merit attention from the media.

In this chapter you will learn how to turn an ordinary venture into an *adventure* — a dramatic, compelling, or exciting event that deserves being mentioned in the media. You will become an expert not only in taking advantage of existing opportunities for free media coverage, but also in creating your own opportunities.

b. LEARN WHAT THE MEDIA WANT

The first step in developing your publicity ideas is understanding what the media want. What events are considered newsworthy

Remember to plan an event that can either educate or entertain the audience (or both!), without turning your publicity into advertising. After all, the basic rule in getting publicity is that you must do something interesting!

enough to be mentioned by the media? What types of activities are frowned on by the press? Here's a quick guide to acceptable practices.

1.   Inform, educate, and entertain

Remember that journalists always need new material to fill the pages of print and hours of broadcast time each day, but there are specific requirements: to inform, to entertain, or to otherwise aid the audience in some way.

Whenever you are considering any promotional undertaking, first ask yourself if it serves the public by informing, educating, or entertaining them. If not, look for a more suitable effort. Remember, too, that if you hope to remain in the limelight for any extended length of time, you won't be able to promote the same event over and over; you'll need to find something fresh in every approach to the press.

2.   No self-serving or hard-sell tactics

Never think of publicity as advertising. A straight sales angle will instantly doom your attempt as far as the media are concerned. Instead, strive for journalistic merit by endowing your promotional activity with either the timeliness of a news event or the warmth and human interest of a feature story. As a rule of thumb, make sure that you're involved in a newsworthy activity, not merely espousing a self-serving cause.

3.   Local angle or national slant

Each medium is interested only in material that is meaningful to its own audience. A nationwide television program, for example, will generally present stories that have national impact, while community newspapers prefer to feature articles with a local slant. The Internet, on the other hand, tends to be organized by topic, rather than region. The next chapter presents a complete picture of how the media industry is structured and what you can do to take advantage of it.

c.   BECOME AN OPPORTUNIST

The basic rule in getting publicity is that you must *do something interesting*. Don't make the mistake of expecting free media exposure simply because you're a nice person and you think your cause is worthy. If you sit back and wait for something to happen, you might wait forever. You need to go out and make it happen.

That doesn't mean you must single-handedly save an entire animal species or invent an amazing new machine. But it does mean that when you're attempting to attract media coverage you need a spark — a catalyst — to get things moving.

When you begin to make plans for your own personalized publicity program, your first option is to become an opportunist. By being constantly aware of what's happening in your local community, in your own field of expertise, and in the mass media, you can make news when there's no news.

One way to get mentioned in the media is to be involved in a news-making story. And even during those slow times when nothing noteworthy is actually happening in your own business, you can generate interest in your enterprise by using the following handy hints for making news.

1. Ride the coattails of a national trend

Ask yourself what fashion trend everyone is talking about; which commodity is in short supply; what the latest food fad is. Then find a way to translate that interest into an opportunity to gain publicity.

Perhaps you could decorate your store to coincide with a country currently in the news; create a display of the newest look in children's clothing; or even dress your employees in costume to celebrate some current event.

For instance, if ecological concerns are in the news and you own a flower shop, perhaps you could arrange an educational window display showing how people can use certain plants to help improve the ecosystem. A computer consultant could piggyback on a national story about "technophobia" by announcing a course on "Overcoming Fear of Computers."

Even non-profit organizations can benefit from this technique. For example, paramedics could turn news stories about the high number of accidental drownings into a fundraiser for water safety seminars. In every case, the main requirement is that the story be associated with some current event and that the promotional activity not be commercially oriented.

2. Use statistics

If you ever notice headlines such as "More than one-fifth of the work force runs a home business" or "Latest study confirms need for senior citizen day care" about your own industry, you can link your publicity efforts to these statistics. Whenever you receive such information in a trade publication or see a similar study in the news, put it in your Publicity Planner for a possible promotional idea.

Alternatively, contact your industry association or government agency and request information that could help you put together a promotional event. A bookstore owner, for example, could quote statistics on illiteracy, and then notify the media that she plans to launch a "Learn to Read" campaign by offering a free story hour once a week. Similarly, a real estate agent could find out how many people fail to quality for home loans and then present a low-cost seminar on "Qualifying for a Home Loan." With the statistics as proof of the problem, the media would probably be happy to help publicize both of these activities.

3. Take part in public events

Major public events that attract thousands of visitors, such as country fairs, automobile shows, and trade expositions, receive plenty of free press by inviting the media to attend. You can get in on that coverage by arranging some special exhibit, display, or demonstration of your own to coincide with the event and then notifying the media of your plans.

Whenever you sign up to participate in such an event, find out who is in charge of publicity. Then call or write that person and ask if you can put on some type of demonstration during the exhibition. If you sell cosmetics, offer to give a free beauty makeover; if you do home improvements, volunteer to demonstrate a woodworking technique; if you are an artist, propose painting a picture during the show and giving it away as a door prize.

If the sponsors of the show are agreeable, work with them to get your name, or the name of your organization, into the publicity material they are sending to the media. That way, when the reporters and photographers show up to cover the day's activities, they'll head right for your display because they'll know about it in advance.

Even if the event's promoters aren't interested in your proposal, you can still take advantage of the opportunity to attract attention. If, for example, you will be displaying your wares in a booth, contact the media in advance of the event and let them know where you'll be located, what you'll be exhibiting, and that you'll be available for an interview.

Events such as country fairs, automobile shows, and trade expositions attract thousands of visitors — and lots of publicity. To tap into this source of publicity, arrange to set up a display at the event, and inform the media.

With publicity there are no guarantees of coverage. But the effort involved in public events is worth the time because journalists assigned to cover these events genuinely appreciate having a little advance information. You might not make it onto the evening newscast every time by following these rules, but you'll sure have a head start.

d. CREATE YOUR OWN OPPORTUNITIES

Your other option is to create your own publicity opportunities. With a little creativity, you can *make* something newsworthy happen. The following ideas illustrate different ways of doing this.

1. Aim for variety

You'll need more than one good idea if you hope to stay in the media spotlight. The key is diversification — constantly creating new opportunities. You can do this by developing a variety of strategies for self-promotion and then targeting different media. For instance, a bookstore owner might plan to issue a press release announcing that a local children's author has won an award and the book is for sale in the store. As a follow-up, the store owner could plan to host the author for an autographing session and invite the local radio or television station to do an interview. The store's Web site should then be updated to highlight the major newsworthy activity, with information about the featured author, and a link to enable Web visitors to order online. To appeal to the TV cameras, the bookstore owner might plan a character look-alike contest for children; and so on.

To make a lasting impression, you have to keep your name before the public on every available front. However, with a little practice, you'll be able to sustain media interest by consistently finding new methods of promoting yourself and your endeavor.

Instead of promoting the same events in the same way year after year, look for new angles or attractions. Take advantage of the times; make your promotions current. In an Olympic year, for example, a candy store might display chocolates in the shape of Olympic medals. Or a real estate office could hold a Halloween celebration in its parking lot and give away free pumpkins to children in costume.

Once you begin your publicity drive in earnest, you won't wish to limit yourself to one or two promotional attempts. Fanning the flames of public attention is exciting and you'll probably find you want to become adept at it.

Continually coming up with new angles for old stories, however, can be tricky unless you know the secrets of attracting attention. On the following pages are suggestions for a number of promotional activities, most of which will work effectively for many different types of pursuits. Study the recommendations, then think about ways in which you can apply them to your own situation.

2. Make things happen

Consider the case of a dry-cleaning firm that had been in business for several years. All but forgotten by the public in favor of newer stores, the owner decided to try generating some interest in his shop. What did he do? He notified the media that he was willing to take donations of old clothes, clean them, and donate them to the homeless people in his town. The result was overwhelming. The dry-cleaning shop was inundated with clothing. The owner was featured in the local newspaper, shown on TV, and interviewed on the radio. By the time the campaign ended, the owner had not only generated a great deal of good will for his store, he had also gained a number of new customers.

Of course, chances are you probably don't own a dry-cleaning company. But similar public-spirited activities are available to everyone hoping to gain access to the media. You only need to know where to find the opportunities and how to take advantage of the possibilities they provide.

3. Consider a community good deed

You will find many positive publicity opportunities if you involve yourself in your community. You must make a sincere commitment if you expect to rely on your standing and reputation over the long run, but if you are willing to give time, energy, and sometimes even money, there are community good deeds to suit every interest.

Begin by examining the options that exist right in your own backyard. Look at your local schools, libraries, charities, and other community associations. First, try to determine which groups most need your help; and second, think about where your own interests lie. To achieve positive results with a campaign like this, you must believe in the cause you have chosen.

After determining which community organization you want to support, make your presence known by volunteering your services in

Using your business to help the community, free of charge, will result in lots of good will and free publicity.

a leadership capacity. You can conduct a clean-up campaign, plant a flower garden, or lead a collection drive.

Be enthusiastic, helpful, and, above all, visible, because although you are working to help a cause, you are also endeavoring to become well known in the community.

Many variations on the community good deed are possible, and, with time, you will probably have a number of innovative ideas of your own. But to get you started in the right direction, here are a few examples of ideas that have worked for others. By no means are they the only available options, but they will serve to give you insight into what you should be striving to achieve.

(a) Adopt a charitable cause

Affiliating with a charity benefits everyone. Not only do you help those in need, but you also profit by creating a positive image in the public eye. Choose a cause you believe in, then make yourself useful by contributing your valuable time or expertise.

One example of this type of activity is to notify your local newspaper that you're challenging the residents of your community to help you raise a certain amount of money for a particular charity. Then, after the money is collected, arrange to donate it in an official ceremony. Later in this book you will receive specific instructions on how to contact the media and interest them in the story of your challenge as well as in the photographs of your ceremony. Suffice it to say that more than one business owner has managed to parlay a similar situation into front-page news.

(b) Set up a beautification committee

For this type of activity, you don't even need to join an existing organization. You can create your own project, complete it, publicize it, and gain a reputation as a hard-working individual who gets things done.

Depending on whether you are seeking local or national attention, your choice of a cause will vary. But as with all good deeds, it is important to choose a goal you believe in and one which makes good use of your talents.

Examples of this type of undertaking include painting the playground equipment at a school, planting chrysanthemums in a park,

As the most savvy and publicity-conscious people know, image is cumulative. Keeping yourself in the public eye adds to your overall recognition.

or building a gazebo in the town square. And once you make up your mind what to do, be sure to notify the media according to the rules you're about to learn (see chapter 4). Remember that when you're engaging in publicity-oriented activities, it's acceptable to take appropriate credit for having originated the idea. Just be sure to mention everyone who helped along the way.

(c) Establish an award

This is a technique that has been used by businesses and nonprofit groups for years to get their names in the news. In fact, many scholarships, tennis tournaments, business awards, and other prizes were actually designed to promote the givers as well as the receivers. Depending on the nature of your own endeavor you, too, might be able to benefit from donating an annual award that recognizes the achievements of others.

Among the practically unlimited possibilities are such honors as "Most Civic-Minded Teenager," "Most Charitable Senior Citizen," or "Best Beautification Project by a Group." You could give a certificate, a trophy, or even a scholarship, but to attract media interest you must be sincere in your presentation and the award must be well deserved.

If you think you might like to donate this type of award, plan to hold a formal presentation ceremony and invite both the public and the press.

4. Try the backdoor approach

Your hobby may be more interesting than your professional career; your office building more interesting than your business. Capitalize on those attention-getting novelties. Don't make the mistake of thinking that all publicity must focus directly on your occupation or your organization.

As the most savvy and publicity-conscious people know, image is cumulative. Keeping yourself in the public eye adds to your overall recognition. And every positive contact with the media adds up to a positive image.

So, go ahead. Promote the fact that you have the community's most extensive collection of tin soldiers or that your home is built on the remains of a Civil War military headquarters. Somewhere along the way, the press coverage will inevitably mention your business or your occupation. Even if the connection isn't direct, getting coverage means you've scored a publicity hit.

One good way to do this is to watch for announcements of upcoming shows, tours, or other public events showcasing such things as historic homes, antique cars, art collections, or even hobbies. For example, if you have a collection, contact the sponsors of a show and see if they would be interested in making your collection part of the exhibit. If so, take advantage of the opportunity to notify the media and steer some of the publicity in your direction. You'll get specific instructions on how to notify the media in chapter 5, "Preparing Publicity Materials: The Press Release."

5. Use the celebrity connection

You don't have to invite an award-winning movie star to your place of business to draw a crowd; local celebrities, including athletes, disc jockeys, and authors, can bring in a lot of people. If you arrange to have a celebrity event, make sure the local news media know about it — in advance. If they're interested in talking to your famous guest, your place of business could show up on the front page.

Authors are usually happy to appear for free anywhere they can autograph and sell copies of their books. But bookstores aren't the only places that profit from such promotions. Cookbook authors attract customers to kitchenware stores, sports writers bring people to sporting good stores, and fashion experts draw crowds to clothing boutiques. One woman who owned a housewares store arranged for a writer to conduct regular workshops right in the store. And a bank had a financial writer sign autographs at the opening of a suburban branch.

Try to contact celebrities such as athletes, journalists, or musicians through their place of employment or their record companies. With writers, it's best to contact them through their publishing companies. And if you ever attend a promotional event where someone famous is appearing, introduce yourself and ask if you might invite them to your place of business as well.

6. Join clubs

Joining clubs, associations, and organizations can afford you quick access to the media spotlight in several different ways. But before you decide which groups to join, think about which ones interest you the most and which might provide you with opportunities for publicity.

Consider business and professional organizations; trade associations; home and garden clubs; sports and recreational groups; and political affiliations. Then choose those that you can help the most and those that can also help you.

Once you become a member, don't just sit back and let the others run things. Volunteer to head a committee, run for office, or set up an event. Better yet, put yourself in charge of generating media coverage for the group. As a spokesperson for your club, you can usually get yourself quoted in the media. And in many cases, your business will be mentioned as well.

7. Be a Web link

Explore the possibilities of getting a link to your Web site from other, compatible Web pages. The people and companies you do business with are a good place to start. Don't be afraid to make contact, and ask about linking up.

8. Use the calendar as a resource

Most people, in their personal lives, look forward to several special days each year — birthdays, anniversaries, holidays. As a businessperson, anticipate special days, too, as a way to promote your company.

(a) Holidays

Certain holidays, of course, are the highlight of retailers' calendars. Some typical holiday publicity attractions include bringing carolers to a store at Christmas, giving away souvenir flags on patriotic holidays, and collecting food for needy families at Thanksgiving.

If you're going to tie your event or promotion to one of the *major* holidays, however, just be aware that there will be a great deal of competition for attention.

(b) Almanacs

What about lesser known "special" days? On Secretary's Day, for instance, an office supply store could give free flowers to office workers. In leap year, on February 29, a jewelry store might hold an unusual timepiece promotion.

If your store promotes lesser known "special" days — such as Secretary's Day — instead of the well known holidays — such as Christmas — you will face less competition for attention and therefore get more press for yourself.

To associate yourself with something out of the ordinary, sit down with a novelty calendar or an almanac and find out what the officially declared commemorative days are. Then choose those that offer you the best chance to promote your business in an unusual way.

(c) Anniversaries

Keep in mind, too, that big news events don't just disappear, they often resurface in "anniversary" stories. "Ten years after the eruption of Mount St. Helen's," for example, practically guaranteed media attention in some parts of the country.

So keep track of major events. When you contact the media about your plans to celebrate that particular anniversary, you will be creating a good opportunity to be featured on the news.

Personal milestones make publicity possibilities as well. Marking your first, tenth, or fiftieth year in business, for example, deserves at least a mention in your local paper's business pages. Some organizations schedule a celebration of their founding every year by putting on a promotional event, such as inviting a local government official to speak at a special ceremony or holding a "birthday" party and inviting the public for cake and ice cream.

Others have found a successful promotional tool in rolling back the price of some popular item to what it was when the business began. Perhaps you could give away an inexpensive replica of something nostalgic that is tied to the anniversary of your organization. Or you could commemorate an unusual fad that was popular the year you started.

(d) Seasonal activities

Every business has its busy season. Because seasonal stories are media favorites, arranging an exceptional promotion might earn you some special press coverage.

But don't think that this type of publicity must be glittery or glamorous. In fact, it frequently works best when it involves plain nuts-and-bolts occurrences. One heating and air-conditioning company, for example, manages to be mentioned twice a year in community newspapers just by offering homeowner hints for preparing equipment to withstand the heat of summer and cold of winter. Similarly, a service station owner gives advice every year to the same reporter about choosing the best tires for winter driving.

Chimney sweeps parade through the pages of newspapers and magazines every year just before cold weather sets in, giving advice on keeping chimneys clean as a safety measure. And a cake decorator calls her neighborhood newsletter every spring to offer a photograph of one of her most romantic wedding cakes for its June cover picture.

(e) Internet events

Whenever you learn of an Internet event that relates to your specialty, such as an upcoming online chat, make sure you note it on your calendar. Then, you can join in the conversation and establish yourself as an expert. At an appropriate time you can refer to your Web site, as a resource.

e. FIFTY PERFECTLY PROMOTABLE IDEAS

In case you need a little help with your creativity, here are 50 suggestions for promotable activities.

1. Arrange an event

- If you have a storefront location, use your imagination to create an unusual exhibit to lure shoppers and then notify the media. Depending on your kind of business, some possible displays include people posing as mannequins, pets available for adoption, a candy-making demonstration, or a fashion show.

- Band together with neighboring business owners and hold a "theme" event, such as "Spring Fling" or "Winter Festival."

- Get together with other artists and crafts people and put on a craft fair. Make it an annual event, include strolling musicians, and add activities for children, and you're practically guaranteed a spot on the six o'clock news.

- Add dash to your grand opening with pipers piping, singers singing, or dancers dancing, and you're more likely to attract attention.

- Sponsor a book-autographing session. A fabric store could host a home-sewing author, a sporting goods outlet might invite an athlete-author, and a children's store could feature a cartoonist. Contact a bookstore or a publisher to arrange selling the author's books on your premises while the author is there.

Remember, events occur on the Internet, too. If you have a Web site, an Internet event provides the perfect opportunity to mention your Web address.

- Hold a wedding in your store, or even in your parking lot. Unusual wedding ceremonies are always being featured in the media.

- Host a Web event, such as an online chat with a celebrity or expert.

- If you are involved in any endeavor that might profit from the clientele of senior citizens, inquire at your local seniors' centers about presenting an educational or entertaining program specifically designed for that sector of the market.

- Plan a celebration to honor your "5,000th customer" or other milestone.

- Proclaim a special week devoted to whatever activity you choose by contacting your local government. In one city, for example, the proprietor of a mystery bookstore convinced the mayor to issue a proclamation calling for "Mystery Readers' Week."

- Hold a contest that features children, such as a humorous photo competition or a "baby race."

- Host a "cook-off" and convince some local celebrities to act as judges.

- Sponsor a health or safety seminar and offer CPR courses or other valuable information.

- Consider off-beat holiday promotions like conducting a gardening lesson on St. Patrick's Day for people who want a "green thumb" or decorating your shop for "Christmas in July."

- If you are seeking donations to support your activities, stage a dramatic presentation showing how your efforts help people, then invite the media and the public to observe.

- For the holiday of your choice, organize a decorated "Holiday House" to raise money for your favorite charity. Include a tea shop, a gift store, or any other enticements the public might like, then notify the media of your plans.

- Hold a fashion show with a theme, such as "Dressing for the Slopes" or "Putting Pizzazz into Pre-School Wardrobes."

Making a donation — whether to an individual, an institution, or your town — is sure to generate some publicity.

◆ Arrange a public service tie-in to your business. Some examples include conducting a blood donor clinic at your store, having police officers available to fingerprint children, or exhibiting the fire department's home safety devices.

◆ Join together with other business owners in your area and arrange for a magician, a clown, or musicians to entertain shoppers during a special promotion marking a holiday or an anniversary.

2.   Make a donation

◆ Hold a draw for a free prize and send a photograph of the winner to your neighborhood "shopper" paper.

◆ Give a scholarship to an exceptional student in the name of your firm.

◆ Mark a patriotic holiday by donating a flag to your town.

◆ Present some needed equipment to a local library, school, seniors' center, or recreation facility.

◆ Offer to award a door prize at any large gathering in which you participate. Make sure your affiliation is mentioned.

◆ If your home town has a museum, donate an artifact for it. But first make sure you set up an attention-getting ceremony to mark the event.

◆ Give away free samples of something related to your business.

◆ Hold a draw for a free prize — the prize could be anything from one of your own products to free tickets to a sporting event. A free prize will undoubtedly draw public interest. Then send an announcement of the winner to your community newspapers.

3.   Give — or get — an award

◆ Honor one of your own employees each month and send the names and photographs of the winners to your local newspaper.

◆ Win an award and let the media know about it.

- Nominate yourself for any awards you are eligible to receive. If you're too modest to name yourself as "Best Person of the Year," have a friend or relative do it for you.

- Take a professional course and, when you complete it, announce your achievement in the press.

4. Make a long-term contribution to your community

- Become a volunteer in your school system.

- Establish a new organization and make yourself the president. It can be social, business, professional, or community, but it should benefit others.

- Offer classes — either free or low-cost — within your place of business. You can teach the sessions yourself or hire an expert. Among the lessons some businesses have presented in the past are Hawaiian dancing, candle making, computer programming, and wallpapering techniques.

- Call your local government and offer to establish an arts program to which you might donate your time or your works.

- Arrange to participate in, or organize, a volunteer program through your local library.

- Learn to speak in sign language and offer your services to hearing-impaired customers by notifying the media.

5. Stand out from the crowd

- Contact every local organization and find out how to get your name listed as a community resource in their telephone directories. The media frequently use these guides as sources for interviews.

- Participate in industry trade shows, keeping your eye out for reporters who happen to be covering the event.

- Plan an auction to raise money for charity, and then volunteer to be the auctioneer.

- Participate in a telethon to raise money for a worthwhile cause. Make every effort to do an outstanding job and you might be featured during the actual television broadcast.

Giving presentations about your field of expertise to local clubs and organizations can be both fun and newsworthy.

◆ Highlight your hobby. Regardless of your business, you can sometimes generate interesting media stories by becoming active in local and national hobby clubs and activities.

◆ Participate in a television game show, and when you return home, offer to tell the media all about your experience.

◆ Whenever you take part in events that are sponsored by others, single yourself out by offering to give a demonstration, conduct a workshop, or hold a prize drawing. Then contact the individual in charge of publicity and make sure that your event is mentioned in the news releases.

◆ Join one or more chambers of commerce, boards of trade, visitors' bureaus, and other business-affiliated organizations. When they sponsor events, be sure you're a visible participant.

6. Speak or write about what you are doing

◆ Speak to clubs and organizations about your field of knowledge. Emphasize consumer hints and provide audience members with some sort of promotional item imprinted with your company name. When approached professionally this can be an especially successful activity. More specific advice is given in chapter 13, "Public Speaking for Publicity and Profit."

◆ Attend an important national or international conference and write an article about it for an industry publication.

◆ Write an advice column for your neighborhood newsletter answering common consumer questions regarding your type of business. Make up two sample columns and present them to an editor for consideration. Always include your Web address. Further instructions are given in chapter 14, "Writing as a Publicity Tool."

◆ Send a consumer hint, or a list of them, to a magazine that publishes such tips. If it's printed, frame it and display it proudly in your place of business.

◆ Offer yourself to an appropriate Web site as a chat guest. Simply send an e-mail message describing yourself as an expert in your field, and volunteer to answer questions live online.

f. ADD TO YOUR PUBLICITY PLANNER

In this chapter you learned how to capitalize on existing events and how to create your own opportunities for publicity. Before you continue, make sure you take the time to note the following information for your Publicity Planner.

1. Promotion ideas

Original ideas, proven ideas, borrowed ideas, creative ideas — all of them need to be written down and put into your "Promotion ideas" folder so you have a wealth of options to choose from when it's time to launch your first campaign.

2. Calendar notes

All of the important events in your business life should be noted on your calendar. Your industry's conventions, your community group's activities, your business anniversaries, and anything else that might be of interest should be recorded for future scheduling purposes. And be sure to include information about possible national tie-ins as well — holidays, sporting competitions, and any upcoming significant events that could offer promotional opportunities.

3. Upcoming events

At this time you'll want to label a file folder for "Upcoming events" to hold all the information, schedules, and plans for upcoming community events — including those organized by other groups — in which you might take part. At the same time, note the date(s) on your calendar.

4
UNDERSTANDING MEDIA ACCESSIBILITY

a. INTRODUCTION

By participating in promotional activities, you plant the seed that will grow into publicity for you and your organization. But to receive publicity, you need the media. Therefore, before you can actually plan a campaign, you must understand how the media are structured so that you can take advantage of the opportunities that exist for coverage.

In this chapter you will become acquainted with the levels of the media, how accessible each level is to you, and how to make the most of the media when planning your publicity campaign. Once you understand how the media work, you'll have a clearer picture of the publicity process.

b. START SMALL

The most common mistake people make in their first attempts at publicity is aiming too high. Don't expect to get exposure on network

Like climbing a mountain, you must start at the bottom when breaking into the media. Deal with the lowest, most accessible levels of media before aiming higher.

television and in national publications with your first effort. You might have heard a few stories of people who have catapulted straight to national attention, but they're too rare to be used as models.

In publicity, like business, there isn't a recipe for "instant success." There are, however, proven methods for accomplishing your goals: aim for realistic targets, then expand your skills to reach the elusive ones. If you had unlimited time and financial resources, you could send your press announcements everywhere. But since you don't, it makes sense to begin by understanding which media are most accessible to beginning publicity-seekers.

To understand the need to "start small" in your publicity program, think of the media as a mountain range. The lowest levels — those that are easiest for a beginning self-promoter to "break into" — are like the foothills. They don't require much effort, but you have to get through them to proceed further up the slope.

As you continue the climb to higher elevations, each level demands a little more expertise and reaching it gives you a little more experience. Finally you get to the summit, the pinnacle for which you were aiming from the beginning. This is an achievement you have to earn. You can no more expect to reach the major media in your first attempt than you could climb Mount Everest without experience.

Working your way through the lower levels of the media toward the summit will give you five major benefits:

(a) You'll learn how the news items that you send to the press are transformed into mentions by the media. Every time you succeed in generating coverage, you'll gain additional insight into what interests journalists and how they make use of your material. In turn, this will give you a head start once you're ready to "climb" into the higher ranks of media exposure.

(b) You'll gain experience in handling interview and online chat situations. Every time you speak to a reporter or other interviewer and then see the result of that conversation in the media, you will learn what to say and what to avoid saying. By building from smaller media outlets to larger arenas, you will have the opportunity to "practice" with small audiences before attempting to make a name for yourself on a national level.

(c) With each success you'll have an addition to your "clippings and quotes" file in your Publicity Planner, which will hold copies of all your media mentions. And as you'll learn in a later chapter, those clippings will become the building blocks on which you will base your "pyramiding" techniques for garnering further publicity.

(d) You'll gain credibility with members of the press each time you are interviewed. If you perform well and give interesting interviews, you'll earn the respect of the media corps, and they'll want to feature you again. It is actually fairly commonplace for journalists and talk-show hosts to get their inspiration for articles and program ideas from other stories they see in the media. With time, yours just might be that story.

(e) Each time you reach new people on the Internet, you multiply your contacts and visibility. You can parlay that into a basic online mailing list for future endeavors.

c. LEVELS OF ACCESSIBILITY IN THE MEDIA

The print, broadcast, and Internet media can be divided into four levels of accessibility. When you're ready to launch your own publicity drive, it will be important for you to remember these levels. For now, simply be aware of the various classifications of the media and how they are ranked. That way, you can target your promotional efforts in a more structured fashion, constantly building your reputation and increasing your visibility.

1. The broadcast media: Radio and television

All broadcasts are not created equal. You can turn the dial on your radio or TV at any time and hear a combination of national programs and local broadcasts. Some will welcome you to participate in their shows; others will receive your message in the mail and politely ignore it.

How do you know when you'll succeed and when you're just spinning your wheels? It's all a question of accessibility. With just a little inside knowledge, you'll understand that it's easier to be on the panel of a local half-hour public affairs TV show than to appear for seven seconds on the national news. And, as you'll discover, one *can* lead to the other, if you know how to make it happen.

(a) Level one: Easy accessibility

The most accessible broadcast outlets for a beginning self-publicist are right in your own backyard — or at least in your own community. They include local cable television stations, low-wattage radio stations, and community announcements on regular TV stations.

Right now, for instance, you could get a message on a local broadcast "bulletin board" by just letting that radio or TV station know what event you want to publicize and where and when it takes place. These stations are especially receptive to events that are open to the public, ones that are either free or very inexpensive. Watch for similar bulletin board announcements — broadcast on radio and TV or sometimes printed across the bottom of the television screen — and use them whenever they are appropriate.

In nearly every North American city that has cable television, there are opportunities for publicity through community access cable programs. This television time is open to anyone who wants to get out a message, as long as the message is not commercial, obscene, or illegal. Cable access is perfect for announcing a fund-raiser, promoting better health and safety practices, offering consumer tips, and generally providing information of interest to the community.

The broadcast time on local access cable television is free, but you might have to do some work to help "produce" your message. That is, you might be asked to make the actual announcement on camera, to read it into the microphone, or to bring in photographs to be shown while the announcement is made. But every station that offers such broadcast time will help guide you through the process, so you'll learn a new skill that might even benefit you in future publicity attempts.

There's more to local broadcasts than just the do-it-yourself programs, however. College radio and TV stations are busy filling hours of on-air time with local guests and participants. These broadcasters are the ones most receptive to your local announcements, your input on community affairs, and your expert advice about your speciality. The same is also true for the television programs produced by volunteers at your community access cable stations. If you can interest them in your topic, you'll probably find yourself being interviewed on local programs more than once.

To be invited to participate in these broadcasts you need only come up with a topic of interest and then notify the stations of your

College radio and TV stations are very receptive to airing announcements, input on community affairs, and expert advice, so go ahead and contact them!

availability as a guest. The trick is to package your proposal properly. The next four chapters will help you prepare your material for presentation to the media.

Do well on local programs and you're likely to be called back. You may even become one of the regulars. The result? You will gain confidence, on-air experience, and a better understanding of what interests broadcasters.

In addition, after you've been on several local broadcasts, you'll learn which questions are asked most often and you'll begin to answer with ease. In other words, you will have taken your first steps up the mountain.

(b) Level two: Moderate accessibility

Local radio and TV programs, produced by a professional staff, may be more difficult to reach, but access is not beyond reasonable expectations. Again, these broadcasters are always looking for participants for their panel discussions or interesting feature stories for their programs.

In many cases the producers or hosts find their guests by listening to and watching other programs or reading about individuals in local newspapers and magazines. These broadcasters are certainly willing to listen to anyone who offers fresh ideas for interesting coverage. The programs most likely to be accessible are the ones called "public affairs" programs, the traditional round table discussions about a topic of interest to the community.

Of course, every locality has its own mix of radio and television broadcasts, and your community may — or may not — have other moderately accessible programs. Among the most common are:

- Very early morning news programs with live interview segments

- Morning talk shows

- Call-in programs that allow listeners or viewers to ask questions of the guest(s)

- Afternoon or early evening newscasts with time devoted to live interviews

- Locally produced talk shows that feature one or more guests at a time

As you climb the media mountain, the competition for space gets tougher. Suddenly, you run into roadblocks and "traps" intended to prevent access to the higher levels.

♦ Community programs focusing on less-than-famous individuals with interesting stories to tell

What makes these programs so accessible to you is that they are produced in the community, for the community. These are not the programs that feature the presidents of international manufacturing firms or the heads of governments. If you can present yourself and your topic in a way that will appeal to the intended audience, you have a good chance of being invited to appear on one or more of these programs.

(c) Level three: Accessibility at the expert level

As you climb the media mountain, the competition for space gets tougher. Suddenly, you run into roadblocks and "traps" intended to prevent access to the higher levels. Major metropolitan broadcasters — talk show emcees and news anchors — simply don't have time to respond to all the requests from people who want to be on their programs. They have to deal with the major issues of the day, so reaching them directly is no longer a possibility.

But there are ways to gain access to this third level of broadcast outlets and their wider audience. One way is through specialty programming — shows that deal with limited topics. These might be nationally syndicated programs or cable television shows. They might be ethnic newscasts or special-interest shows (on dogs, say, or gardening) or programs that focus on a narrow topic such as trout fishing. Many of these programs are looking for guests who know about a specific field.

Some of these shows are done at the major metropolitan television and radio stations; others are put together at private facilities called production houses. Whenever you notice a special-interest show for which you believe you are qualified, call and get the producer's name so you can inquire about appearing. But make sure you've made it high enough on the mountain to have earned a position on the program first.

But remember, this is not for media beginners. You need to have experience before you make that call. You'll want to know what kinds of things broadcasters respond to. Success at levels one and two will give you that experience.

At this level of accessibility are the major programs in your area that draw celebrities and prominent people as guests. These programs are higher profile and more competitive. To convince the producers to include you, you must have a message of widespread interest and the ability to convey it. Individuals who are invited onto these programs usually have a good track record. The producers have usually seen them being interviewed or read about them and have confidence that "this guest can handle the demands of our broadcast."

Major newscasts in your area might be slightly more accessible than celebrity shows. In large cities, the television and radio news programs touch on many topics besides news, often including human interest and feature stories. If you have a story that attracts the attention of broadcasters at this level, the producer will sometimes "check out" your story by sending a video crew or a reporter. Even a very brief appearance can actually be your "audition" for longer programs and lead up to the next level.

(d) Level four: The big time

The national media, from network newscasts to national talk shows, are the very peak of the media mountain. And although you can consider appearances on national programs as long-term goals, don't waste energy trying to get there until you've mastered the media at the lower levels first.

As a rule, the national media simply are not directly accessible to small businesses, individual professionals, or local organizations. Producers for these programs can turn to the most renowned experts on any subject. Why should they spend time conducting "pre-interviews" to determine if a self-employed bridal consultant would be a suitable guest when the managing editor of the biggest international bridal magazine is available? Which one carries more weight with the public? Which is the proven winner?

If it is your goal to reach this level of media exposure, you will have to make publicity your single most important focus. You will need to start with small outlets and work your way to the bigger ones until you *are* the nationally known expert in your field.

A major news event *might* fall into your lap. Don't put it outside the realm of possibilities. But it is unlikely that you will get to the national broadcast arena until you are truly a media expert.

2. Print media

Print publications can also be divided into categories by levels of accessibility. While you can easily place an announcement in your homeowners' association newsletter, for example, you would probably find it extremely difficult to persuade a national magazine to do a feature article on your business.

However, once you have been showcased in the local print media, you can use that experience to approach more prestigious publications.

(a) Level one: Easy accessibility

When you think about publicity, never overlook any local sources that might mention you in print. These include club newsletters, church bulletins, local business association newsletters, neighborhood announcements, or any other small publications of only a few pages. Most of them don't have room for long messages, but you can certainly make use of them to publicize your new business, fund-raising activity, or professional award.

Equally accessible for first-time self-promoters are high school and college alumni magazines. In fact, most of them are begging for submissions and frequently publish a request for information. One woman who brought herself to the attention of her university's magazine was featured in a half-page story in which she managed to mention her new service business six times.

(b) Level two: Moderate accessibility

Many print outlets must be classified as moderately accessible because although they will publish as many announcements as they have room for, they receive too much promotional material to feature everyone who wants to be mentioned.

Weekly newspapers, community papers, local trade association publications, and the newsletters of national business and social organizations are all moderately accessible. To be chosen for coverage, you need to have an especially interesting tale to tell. To make yourself more appealing to these publications, remember that the more community oriented and less commercial your story is, the more likely you are to be singled out for special treatment.

(c) Level three: National special-interest publications

Special-interest publications are a growing source of accessible publicity. These publications can be either newspapers or magazines, but they always focus on one subject, such as mysteries, antiques, crafts, birds, hobbies — the list is very long. All special-interest publications have one thing in common: the editors welcome input from readers. You can probably break into print fairly easily with a letter to the editor or a handy hint about something in your field. If you have your heart set on a feature article, however, you must have climbed far enough up the media mountain that you rank as a specialist in your field.

National trade publications, association magazines, and professional journals such as those devoted to the business of builders, lawyers, or accountants are also fairly high on the media mountain. They, too, have a long list of experts to interview when they prepare feature stories. Once you've been written up in several of your home town publications, however, these publications tend to look more favorably on you.

(d) Level four: Big-city newspapers and national magazines

You'll know you've reached the top of the print mountain when you're featured in major metropolitan newspapers, national news magazines, or best-selling general interest magazines. Their writers and reporters keep files of interview sources that include the top experts in each field.

Whether you're an author, a business owner, an athlete, a musician, or a consultant, you must earn your place on their pages. And the best way to accomplish that is to make publicity a part of your overall program for success. After you've been mentioned in all of the lower levels of the media, the top-ranking print journalists will start calling you, too.

3. World Wide Web

Like the other media, the Internet offers different levels of exposure, depending on your resourcefulness, and experience. Working your way up on the World Wide Web can lead to international visibility and all the benefits that entails.

(a) Level one: Easy accessibility

The most basic step in your Internet efforts is the creation of your own Web site, touting your organization, products, or expertise. Web sites can be as simple or elaborate as you have the time and ability to make them. But even the simplest Web page must be graphically appealing and user friendly. And above all, update, update, update. It can be disappointing to your visitors to see that you haven't kept up with current ideas and events. You lose points, and maybe even future visitors.

(b) Level two: Moderate accessibility

Reach out beyond your own Web address. One way to do that is to establish links with other Web sites. You can also add links to related topics from your site. That way your site becomes a more valuable resource to visitors.

And, you can get more involved through online chats. Such chat opportunities are not the place for hard sell tactics, but you can promote yourself or your group, by referring to your product or organization when it's appropriate. Remember, you are trying to be helpful and informative.

(c) Level three: Search engines

Search engines can draw people to the latest article or discussion on your Web site. It could be worth your time to investigate the best ways to get listed prominently on the most popular search engines. Make sure you keep current, and appear under as many headings as possible.

(d) Level four: The major home pages

On the World Wide Web, the highest degree of exposure comes from the Internet Service Providers that have the most subscribers. Getting a link on the home page of one of these ISPs can send your visibility to new heights. Once you've established your own Web page, with links to and from other Web sites, and are listed on some significant search engines, you're ready to start aiming for the big time.

To begin getting publicity on the Internet, build a Web site. Remember to update it frequently, to show that you're staying on top of current events.

d. WORK YOUR WAY UP

Getting publicity means seeking media attention for your business, your cause, or yourself. But as you strive for that attention, keep in mind that because of the way the media are structured you must work your way up from the lowest levels of accessibility to the highest.

This knowledge will help you save time and effort you might otherwise waste by aiming at inappropriate targets. By planning ahead and building your program in an organized fashion, you stand a better chance of achieving success.

As you climb the mountain that represents achievement in the media, spend time at every level because *all* publicity is valuable. Each time your name is mentioned, you gain — whether it is public recognition, new customers, or additional contributors.

Learn all you can before you move higher, and when you reach the top, your achievement will be even more meaningful because you will know how many obstacles you've overcome to get to your goal.

5
PREPARING PUBLICITY MATERIALS: THE PRESS RELEASE

a. INTRODUCTION

After you have made some decisions about possible promotional activities, and once you are familiar with the concept of media accessibility, it's time for the next step in the publicity process: notifying the media. Because the competition for coverage is intense, it is important to understand the rules for contacting the press.

The single most important tool for communicating with the media is the press release, or news release as it is also known. Everyone who wants to generate publicity needs to know how to write a press release. If you are hoping for high visibility, promoting yourself to the media is not only acceptable, it is imperative. Business owners, consultants, magicians, artists, authors, musicians, and even nonprofit organizations are no longer sitting back and waiting to be noticed. They are taking the initiative by sending attention-getting press releases, and so can you.

This chapter will explain the purpose of a press release, how to write press releases for all occasions, and ways to make your press releases stand out from the rest. A worksheet will aid you in composing your own releases and samples will serve as guidelines for you to follow.

Then, because press releases are such an integral part of any publicity effort, later chapters in the book will address related topics, including where to send your press releases, sources for finding names and addresses, instructions for following up on your mailings, when to send your announcements, and how to incorporate them into your overall publicity program.

Although writing press releases on a regular basis may sound daunting to you now, be assured that the step-by-step directions provided in this chapter were especially designed to turn you into an expert. By adhering to a few simple rules, you will soon be sending press releases that have what it takes to gain positive publicity for you and your organization.

b. WHAT IS A PRESS RELEASE?

By definition a press release is simply a statement prepared for distribution to the media. In appearance it looks like a business letter, while in content it more closely resembles a newspaper article.

Like a letter, a press release is a message typed on business stationery. It is usually no more than one or two pages long and it is sent to individual members of the media — most often to print editors, broadcast producers, and television news assignment editors.

But unlike a letter, a press release never includes a salutation or a signature. It is an impersonal, straightforward statement about your activities.

The purpose of a press release is to give journalists information that is useful, accurate, and interesting. It represents your first contact with the press *each time* you hope to be mentioned in the media.

Whenever you open a new office, win an award, sponsor a significant event, plan an unusual celebration, reach a milestone, or introduce a unique product, you deserve recognition. To gain that recognition and to start the publicity ball rolling, you need to notify the media.

The press release is the single most important tool for communicating with the media. Its purpose is to give journalists information that is useful, accurate, and interesting.

Although you might be tempted to place a phone call or write a letter, use a press release. This is the method of communication that the media expect and are best equipped to handle. It doesn't matter if your goal is a brief announcement in the pages of a neighborhood newsletter, exposure on the evening news, an article in your daily paper, or a guest spot on a TV talk show, the place to start is by sending a press release.

The use of press releases has become so widespread in the media today that dozens of them arrive daily at even the smallest newspapers and radio stations. Major media outlets receive hundreds of releases daily. In fact, industry insiders estimate that nearly half of what passes for news today actually originated as a press release.

Now turn to Sample 1 to see what an actual press release looks like.

c. RULES FOR WRITING PRESS RELEASES

Press releases must conform to an established format because, with so many arriving daily, journalists don't have time to wade through material that has been improperly prepared. You must meet their expectations if you hope to have your releases read. Once you become familiar with the form, however, you won't find it difficult to write press releases because they all follow the same basic pattern, regardless of subject matter. The following guidelines will help you prepare press releases according to the basic pattern.

1. Style

In theory, the press release is your opportunity to tell the media all about your latest endeavor. But in practice, it is not actually written from your personal point of view. Instead, it is prepared by you as if you were a newspaper reporter interviewing yourself. Intended to be printed or broadcast in the media exactly "as is," without changing even one word, a press release must be written in journalistic style from start to finish.

For this reason, you must always refer to yourself in the third person — as "he" or "she" — in your own press releases. The personal pronouns "I," "me," and "mine" should never appear in an announcement unless you are actually quoting yourself and your statement is set apart in quotation marks.

SAMPLE 1
PRESS RELEASE

ANYCOMPUTER COMPANY
0000 Raincloud Street
Anycity, Anystate 00000
Telephone: (555) 555-5555
Fax: (555) 555-1111
E-mail: Aanyone@anycomputer.com

PRESS RELEASE

April 1, 20—
For Immediate Release

Contact: Albert Anyone
Days: (555) 555-5555
Evenings: (555) 555-1212
E-mail: Aanyone@anycomputer.com

Anycomputer Company Offering Free Workshops

Albert Anyone, president of Anycomputer Company in Anycity, Anystate, has announced a series of free computer workshops to be held at the Anycomputer store at 555 Middle Street beginning Monday, April 24, 20—.

An introductory course designed for those who want basic information, the two-hour workshops will be conducted from 7 p.m. to 9 p.m. on Mondays and Thursdays only. Topics to be covered include selecting software, getting the most out of word processing, using spreadsheets, making an address book, and using search engines. Teachers will include Mr. Anyone as well as company sales counselors Sam Samms and Brenda Brenn.

-more-

Computer

A graduate of Anystate University with a degree in computer engineering, Mr. Anyone founded Anycomputer Company in 1999 and has earned several industry awards for his firm's innovative programs in consumer education.

Reservations are required for the computer workshops. For further information or reservations phone (555) 555-5555 or visit the Web site, anycomputer.com.

-end-

Your press release will be competing with many other pieces of mail for a journalist's attention, so make sure it is neat, professional looking, and easy to read.

In addition, you need to begin with the most important facts, follow up with slightly less important information, and end with the least important data. That way, if the editor has to shorten your statement, the last sentences or paragraphs can be cut without losing the main impact of the announcement.

2. Appearance

The appearance of your press release is important because it must compete with many other pieces of mail for a journalist's attention. It pays, therefore, to make your missives as attractive as possible. Proper appearance doesn't mean an expensively printed product on high-gloss paper, though. All that is required is a neatly typed notice that shows you have paid attention to preparation. Sloppy presentation tells the recipient that you don't care very much about the way your company appears to others. And if you don't care, why should anyone else?

Pay attention to the following three aspects of appearance: the design of your letterhead, the legibility of the printing, and the layout of the page.

(a) Letterhead

Always print your press releases on business letterhead stationery pre-printed with the name, address, Internet addresses, and phone numbers of your organization. If you are sending a fax, make sure your letterhead will reproduce well. For e-mails, keep your design simple to minimize the recipient's wait time, and maximize their first impression.

(b) Legibility

Print all your announcements in easy-to-read, standard font styles. Avoid the elaborate or gimmicky styles, which are too hard to read. Because members of the media are required to do a great deal of reading, they prefer clear, sharply produced type rather than exotic print styles.

(c) Layout

Keep the layout simple and easy to read. Stick with one font style for the body of the news release, and use a standard style size font: 12 to 14 points is the preferred size. Allow margins of at least one inch on every side. Also, for visual appeal, center the information on the page.

3. Writing headlines

Don't underestimate the importance of the headline on your news release, or the subject line if you're sending e-mail. Strive to capture the recipient's imagination so that he or she will want to read the rest of the release. A headline that grabs the reader's attention can help catapult your news release into a front-page feature story.

Although writing headlines is an art, you can pick up some of the techniques by perusing your daily newspaper for clues. And even though the headline you create will probably never be seen by the public because most people in the media prefer to write their own, a headline can be helpful in making the media take notice.

But if you just can't come up with a short, snappy statement, here are four quick tricks to help.

(a) Practice alliteration

"Pet Pooch Ponders Prestigious Prize" could headline a press release announcing an award won by a business owner's dog. (This is also an example of using the "backdoor approach" to getting your name in the news.)

(b) Make use of a pun

Some situations seem to lend themselves ideally to a humorous play on words, such as, "Candy Maker Knows Sweet Smell of Success."

(c) Offer "inside" secrets or consumer hints

"Boomtown Bridal Store Owner Offers Secrets of Wedding Success" or "Raintown Electrician Holds Seminar on Hidden Household Hazards" would probably attract more attention than such plain statements as "Bridal Store Sells Wedding Dresses" or "Raintown Electrician Wants Your Business."

(d) Use a colon

This simple shorthand technique allows you to state the subject of your press release right up front in one or two words. A financial consultant announcing the opening of a new office might write, "Financial Consulting: Mytown Resident Offers a New Perspective." Or an appliance store owner could introduce a new product with the headline, "Dishwashers: Mycity Store Owner Introduces the Latest Look."

Keep your press releases brief and easy to read.

4. Grammar and format

Press releases are subject to the normal rules of standard English grammar from paragraphing to punctuation. Because those submissions that require the least editing are the ones most likely to be used, you'll boost your chances for success by following these suggestions:

(a) Be brief. One page is the preferred length, two the maximum. If reporters want more information, they will call or e-mail you.

(b) Use simple, declarative sentences and avoid flowery language. Don't use five words when one will do. If you put your facts in order, you'll find that your announcement practically writes itself.

(c) State your information in a straightforward fashion by sticking to facts and avoiding personal opinions. Never say "Cloudburst Car Wash is the best in town" or "You'll love the service at Tock's Clock Shop" because those are statements of opinion. Instead, say "Tock's Clock Shop has been in business since 1948," or "Cloudburst Car Wash was honored for its on-time performance by the car wash industry." Those are facts.

(d) In references to the time of day, always include either a.m. or p.m. in lowercase letters. The only exceptions are 12:00 midnight and 12:00 noon, which should be written simply as "midnight" and "noon."

(e) Never abbreviate the first time you refer to something or someone, except for a.m., p.m., and titles, such as Dr. It's acceptable to abbreviate in a second reference. For example, spell out the name and add initials in parentheses the first time you refer to the "Neighborhood Beautification and Enhancement Committee (NBEC)," but in the next mention use only the initials, NBEC.

(f) The first time you refer to an individual, spell out the entire name, such as Dr. William Wellness. After that, the appropriate title and the last name only may be used (Dr. Wellness).

(g) Use the names of both the city and the state or province when referring to a location.

(h) Whenever you mention a day, be sure to write the date, including the year. Unfortunately, in some newsrooms, old press releases have surfaced long after their intended date for publication and accidentally been printed. Including the year can help to prevent any unexpected problems.

(i) Never use insider jargon. Words that have meaning in one particular industry are often meaningless to the general public.

5. A sample layout

Although press releases will vary from event to event and from writer to writer, all of them should conform to the standard layout illustrated in Sample 2. Features of this layout that you should particularly note are indicated in the sample by letters in parentheses — (a), (b), (c), and so on. An explanation of each feature can be found in the following text:

(a) Always use business letterhead with the name, address, telephone numbers, and Internet address of your firm or organization. This not only adds an air of legitimacy to your endeavor, it also provides the recipient with the correct spelling of your organization's name, your address, and your telephone numbers.

(b) Print press releases on one side of the paper only, with margins of at least one inch all the way around.

(c) Begin your message by centering the words "PRESS RELEASE" (all in capital letters) approximately two lines below the business heading.

(d) Two lines below the words PRESS RELEASE, type the date at the left-hand margin.

(e) If your announcement may be published right away, type "For Immediate Release" directly below the date. If you would like the information held or "embargoed" until a specific date, type "For Release After (fill in the date, including the year)." Just be aware that not all media will honor an embargo.

(f) On the same line as the date, beginning in the center of the page, type the name of the person the media may contact for more information, as follows: "Contact: (Fill in the first and last names)." If you are self-employed, you will undoubtedly want to be the contact person. If you are part of a large organization or coalition, however, you need to designate an official spokesperson before you send out your first release.

SAMPLE 2
PRESS RELEASE — LAYOUT

ANYCOMPUTER COMPANY
0000 Raincloud Street
Anycity, Anystate 00000
Telephone: (555) 555-5555   (a)
Fax: (555) 555-1111
E-mail: Aanyone@anycomputer.com

(b)

PRESS RELEASE   (c)

(d) April 1, 20—   Contact: Albert Anyone   (f)
(e) For Immediate Release   Days: (555) 555-5555   (g)
                                                 Evenings: (555) 555-1212 (h)
                                   E-mail: Aanyone@anycomputer.com   (i)

Anycomputer Company Offering Free Workshops   (j)

(k)   Albert Anyone, president of Anycomputer Company in Anycity,
Anystate, has announced a series of free computer workshops to be held   (l)
at the Anycomputer store at 555 Middle Street beginning Monday,
April 24, 20—.

   An introductory course designed for those who want basic information,
the two-hour workshops will be conducted from 7 p.m. to 9 p.m. on   (m)
Mondays and Thursdays only. Topics to be covered include selecting
software, getting the most out of word processing, using spreadsheets,
making an address book, and using search engines. Teachers will include
Mr. Anyone as well as company sales counselors Sam Samms and Brenda
Brenn.   (q)

                              -more-   (r)

Sample 2 — Continued

(u) ——

(s) Computer

2 (t)

A graduate of Anystate University with a degree in computer engineering, Mr. Anyone founded Anycomputer Company in 1999 and has (n) earned several industry awards for his firm's innovative programs in consumer education.

Reservations are required for the computer workshops. For further (o) information or reservations phone (555) 555-5555 or visit the Web site, anycomputer.com.

-end- (p)

And it must be understood that the person you choose has the authority of the organization to speak with members of the media in representing the group.

(g) Directly underneath the name of the contact person, type that person's daytime telephone number, including the area code, as follows: "Days: (555) 555-5555."

(h) On the next line, directly below the daytime number, type that person's evening telephone number, as follows: "Evenings: (555) 555-1212."

(i) On the next line, provide the e-mail address that will be used. Make sure it is an address from which mail is retrieved frequently.

(j) Skip a line and type a one-line headline to help the recipient understand the subject of your release.

(k) Double-space and begin your announcement, indenting all paragraphs.

(l) In the first paragraph, the writing should conform to basic newswriting style, telling who, what, where, and when.

(m) The next paragraph should include a brief description of the project, event, company, or product being promoted, including any facts pertaining to its significance.

(n) The third paragraph should be a concise biography of the main individual involved.

(o) When suitable, end with the sentence, "For more information, contact (fill in name) at (555) 555-5555."

(p) At the end of the announcement, below the final sentence and centered between the right and left edges, type "-end-."

If your release is longer than one page —

(q) Don't break a paragraph or sentence at the bottom of a page. Just rearrange the material to look nicely centered on the first page and begin again at the top of the second page.

(r) Type "-more-" at the bottom of each page to indicate that there are more pages.

(s) At the top of every page except the first, type a one-word heading — one line below the top of the page and one inch from the left-hand edge of the paper — to identify your release in case the pages become separated after they reach the media. Typically, the heading should be either the name of the event or organization that is the subject of the release, such as "Fair" or "Cakes."

(t) Number the pages consecutively at the top. It is not necessary, however, to number the first page.

(u) Staple the pages together.

If you adhere to these instructions, you can be confident that your press releases will look their best and receive the most consideration.

Now it is time to practice writing your first press release. First, use Worksheet 3 to organize your material. Then write your press release using the format outlined in Sample 2.

d. ALWAYS DOUBLE CHECK

When you send a press release, it signals three things to the recipient: you have a newsworthy announcement; you have taken the time to present your information clearly and concisely; and you are ready to answer further questions on the subject.

Don't take any chances on losing your opportunity for press coverage. Before you send your messages to the media, make sure they're correct in every detail. There is nothing worse than having to call a newsroom and explain that an error exists in your announcement. Not only is it embarrassing, it can be very costly, because the reporters you call will probably never trust your releases again.

Even if you think your press release is technically perfect, always proofread your final copy one last time. A high quality product can be your key to fame and fortune. Checklist 1 has been designed to help you review your press releases. Taking the time to double check your work can pay off in the end.

e. TIPS TO MAKE YOUR PRESS RELEASES SPARKLE

Now that your first press release is written, take a critical look at it. Is it interesting? Does it make you want to read on? Remember, your press release is competing with many others for attention in the newsroom. You need to add a little "oomph!"

How can you do this? Members of the media always want to know what's unique, special, or different about your story. Learn to emphasize what makes *your* event notable. Are you giving an award

Always proofread your press release carefully before sending it to the media. Mistakes can cost you your reputation with reporters!

WORKSHEET 3
WRITING A PRESS RELEASE

Each time you need to send a press release, begin by writing down the answers to the questions below.

1. What is the main point you want to make in your press release?

    _____

2. What are the major elements of your story?

    Who? _____

    What? _____

    Where? _____

    When? _____

    How? _____

    Why? _____

3. If you are introducing a new product, selling a service, or sponsoring an event, how much does it cost?

    _____

4. Are there any special features (e.g., free admission for children under 12 or discounts on food for senior citizens)?

    _____

5. What are the activities you have planned and the specific hours for each?

    _____

    _____

    _____

6. Are there any restrictions?

    _____

7. What are the other newsworthy aspects of this event, activity, or announcement?

    _____

    _____

CHECKLIST 1
REVIEW YOUR PRESS RELEASE

Before you send your press releases, review this list to make sure you have prepared them properly.

1. Did you use letterhead?

2. Have you included the release date and contact person?

3. Does the page look neat and visually balanced?

4. Have you stated the four basic facts — who, what, where, and when — in the first paragraph?

5. Is there a genuine newsworthiness or public interest element to your announcement?

6. Have you proofread for spelling, grammar, punctuation, and accuracy?

to the oldest or youngest person in the field? Are you starting a company in the "fastest-growing sector of the industry?" Do you offer the "only service of its kind within 200 miles?"

Sample 3 is an example of a news release that highlights the uncommon aspects of an automobile exhibit. Note the use of the words "unusual," "first," and "unique" in the release. These are the kind of words that catch a journalist's attention.

As you read Sample 3, and others throughout the book, watch for the phrases that add sparkle. They generally fall into four categories.

1. Factual superlatives

Be sure you are accurate, but if you can honestly describe your event or product as the largest, the smallest, the newest, the oldest, even the second largest, or *one* of the oldest, you will make your story stand out.

2. Quotes and reactions

Quotations and reaction statements add color, because they are the only acceptable way to use subjective language and exclamations. Without quotes in a news release, for example, you would be limited to stating, "Miss Smith-Smythe received the annual Garden Club award." On the other hand, by quoting yourself you could write, "Miss Smith-Smythe accepted the annual Garden Club award saying,

SAMPLE 3
BASIC PRESS RELEASE

AUTO CAR RESTORATION INC.
1234 RUN ROAD
OURTOWN, NEBRASKA 00000
Telephone: (555) 555-2222
Fax: (555) 555-1111
E-mail: aauto@autocarrestoration.com

PRESS RELEASE

May 5, 20—   Contact: Albert Auto
For Immediate Release   Days: (555) 555-2222
                                              Evenings: (555) 555-1212
                              E-mail: aauto@autocarrestoration.com

The Oldest Traffic Jam in Town

As 150 antique automobiles converge on Market Square in Ourtown, Nebraska, for a weekend exhibit, it will look like a traffic jam out of the past. Scheduled for Saturday and Sunday, May 27 and 28, 20—, from 10 a.m. to 5 p.m., the two-day event will feature a number of unusual models.

Original Quantum Cars — polished to look like new — will be displayed side-by-side with the first luxury automobile to cost more than $2,000, the Zinger. The antique passenger coaches in this special reunion will average 50 years of age, with the oldest a 1937 Running Roadster.

-more-

Sample 3 — Continued

Cars

2

    The unique gathering was organized by Albert Auto, a local craftsman who combines his love of antiquated cars with his career of restoring their original appearance. Mr. Auto, owner of Auto Car Restoration of Ourtown, Nebraska, says that the event will be exceptional because several of the featured cars are one-of-a-kind models.

    For further information, contact Albert Auto at (555) 555-2222 or visit the Web site, autocarrestoration.com.

-end-

`This is the best thing that's happened to me since I won the National Spelling Competition in tenth grade!'"

So try to include quotes, even if you are the one being quoted and you have to spend an hour coming up with a clever phrase. And should you be interviewed as a result of sending the press release, it's perfectly acceptable to repeat the same remark as though it were spontaneous. More often than not, it's exactly what reporters want to hear.

Refer to Samples 4 and 5 to see how quotes add interest to two more news releases about the automobile exhibit.

3. Details

Exactly what is it that makes your news unusual? You might have to do some creative thinking to find a new angle or a little-known detail, but that added piece of information can help "sell" your story.

To help "sell" your story, try to think of a new angle or little-known detail that will make your news unusual.

One example is the real estate agent who wanted to use publicity to attract new customers. When he earned an award as the top first-year salesperson in his office and he notified the media of his achievement, he suggested two other story angles.

First, he explained that he was a senior citizen who had already retired from one successful career as a business executive.

And second, he mentioned his museum-quality collection of antique doorknobs which he had been assembling for most of his life.

These two additional details were enough to convince the media to feature him in a story.

4. Human interest

Sometimes including a few words about someone's personal life can spark media interest. An editor might not care a great deal about an award being given, but if there's something unusual about the recipient (he or she was a political refugee, the sole survivor of a major catastrophe 20 years ago, etc.), mentioning it in your news release could be reason enough to get coverage.

Try to find that element with every release you send and you'll improve your success rate.

SAMPLE 4
PRESS RELEASE USING QUOTES

AUTO CAR RESTORATION INC.

1234 RUN ROAD
OURTOWN, NEBRASKA 00000
Telephone: (555) 555-2222
Fax: (555) 555-1111
E-mail: aauto@autocarrestoration.com

PRESS RELEASE

May 5, 20—
For Immediate Release

Contact: Albert Auto
Days: (555) 555-2222
Evenings: (555) 555-1212
E-mail: aauto@autocarrestoration.com

The Oldest Traffic Jam in Town

As 150 antique automobiles converge on Market Square in Ourtown, Nebraska, for a weekend exhibit, it will look like a traffic jam out of the past. Scheduled for Saturday and Sunday, May 27 and 28, 20—, from 10 a.m. to 5 p.m., the two-day event will feature a number of unusual models.

Original Quantum Cars — polished to look like new — will be displayed side-by-side with the first luxury automobile to cost more than $2,000, the Zinger. The antique passenger coaches in this special reunion will average 50 years of age, with the oldest a 1937 Running Roadster.

-more-

Cars

2

The unique gathering was organized by Albert Auto, a local craftsman who combines his love of antiquated cars with his career of restoring their original appearance.

"The stories behind many of these cars are just incredible," Auto says, recounting the story of the one which received the most careful maintenance. "It was owned for 25 years by the only obstetrician in town. And that doctor never missed one birth due to car problems."

Mr. Auto, owner of Auto Car Restoration of Ourtown, Nebraska, notes that admission to the automobile jamboree is free. "And the local fire department auxiliary will be selling refreshments," he says.

For further information, contact Albert Auto at (555) 555-2222 or visit the Web site, autocarrestoration.com.

-end-

AUTOMOTIVE SHOWROOM

4321 PLAZA SQUARE
BIG CITY, KANSAS 00000
Telephone: (555) 555-4321
Fax: (555) 555-1111
E-mail: mmycar@automotiveshowroom.com

PRESS RELEASE

May 6, 20—   Contact: Mary Mycar
For Immediate Release   Days: (555) 555-4321
                                                   Evenings: (555) 555-6789
                              E-mail: mmycar@automotiveshowroom.com

One-of-a-Kind Palomino Motor Car on Display

A rare Palomino Motor Car will be among the unusual vehicles on display at the antique auto show to be held May 27 and 28, 20—, at Market Square in Anytown. The car — still shining in its original Midnight Blue color — has the features that made the Palomino the phenomenon of 1945: the mahogany dashboard with fluorescent instrument panel, the molded fiberglass seats, and the chinchilla carpet.

The owner of the Palomino, Mary Mycar, who operates Automotive Showroom in Big City, Kansas, says that her car is a particular source of pride for her. "It has a wonderful history of loving care that really sets it apart. All of its original features have been carefully restored and are nearly as fine as when they were first installed."

-more-

Sample 5 — Continued

Cars

2

At the auto jamboree, which will be free and open to the public from 10 a.m. to 5 p.m. both days, Miss Mycar will also exhibit nine other antiquated autos ranging in age from a 1949 Unicorn to a 1956 Raycar.

"It will be a fun event, even for people who don't collect old cars," she says. "I hope everyone will come out and bring the whole family."

For more information, contact Mary Mycar at (555) 555-4321, or visit the Web site, automotiveshowroom.com.

-end-

f. DIFFERENT MEDIA, DIFFERENT SLANT

When you write a press release for the print media, which includes not only newspapers and magazines, but also smaller publications like newsletters, alumni bulletins, and community "shopper" papers, you should approach the subject as if you were a newspaper reporter by emphasizing the news aspect and the facts. That way, the press can print your announcement "as is."

For radio and television, however, two other factors need to be considered: sound and sight. Even though it is not strictly necessary to write different press releases every time for every medium, when you are actively pursuing major publicity coverage you can slant your press releases slightly to appeal to the different kinds of media.

For Internet distribution, your news release might include additional references as well as links to other Internet sites. The more helpful your information is, the more likely you will be regarded as a valuable resource.

Turn to Sample 6 and Sample 7 for examples of how to add some aural and visual interest to the press releases announcing the auto exhibit. Then think about similar possibilities inherent in your own promotional activities.

g. THE FIVE FATES OF THE PRESS RELEASE

Not every press release will draw the publicity you want. Sometimes that's your fault, sometimes it's not. To understand how to make the most of your efforts, you'll need to know what happens to your press releases after they leave your hands. Basically there are five possible fates of the press material you send, from immediate rejection to overwhelming acceptance.

There are five possible fates of your press release, from being tossed in the trash to making the big time.

1. Fate number one: Tossed in the trash can

The worst thing that can happen to a press release is to be read and tossed immediately into the trash, or deleted from the recipient's inbox. The most common reasons for rejections are the following:

(a) The announcement is too late to meet the deadline. This can be remedied by noting deadline information in your Publicity Planner.

AUTO CAR RESTORATION INC.

1234 RUN ROAD
OURTOWN, NEBRASKA 00000
Telephone: (555) 555-2222
Fax: (555) 555-1111
E-mail: aauto@autocarrestoration.com

PRESS RELEASE

May 5, 20—   Contact: Albert Auto
For Immediate Release   Days: (555) 555-2222
                                        Evenings: (555) 555-1212
                          E-mail: aauto@autocarrestoration.com

Old Sounds Come Back to Life

The purr of a mint-condition Palomino Motor Car, the howl of the horn on a Luxury Lance.... Market Square in Ourtown, Nebraska, will bring back the sounds of yesteryear with an exhibit of antique autos on Saturday and Sunday, May 26 and 27, 20–, from 10 a.m. to 5 p.m.

Thanks to organizer Albert Auto, the owner of Auto Car Restoration Inc. in Ourtown, 150 cars will be on display. And although the gathering will last only two days, Mr. Auto says interest in the cars spans several generations.

Admission to the event is free and refreshments will be available, provided by the Ourtown Fire Department Auxiliary. For more information, contact Albert Auto at (555) 555-2222 or visit the Web site, autocarrestoration.com.

-end-

AUTOMOTIVE CAR RESTORATION, INC.
1234 RUN ROAD
OURTOWN, NEBRASKA 00000
Telephone: (555) 555-2222
Fax: (555) 555-1111
E-mail: aauto@autocarrestoration.com

PRESS RELEASE

May 5, 20—
For Immediate Release

Contact: Albert Auto
Days: (555) 555-2222
Evenings: (555) 555-1212
E-mail: aauto@autocarrestoration.com

Sights and Sounds of the Past Come to Life

It will look like a scene created by Hollywood, but it won't be a re-creation, it will be an original. More than 150 antique automobiles will be on display Saturday and Sunday, May 26 and 27, 20—, at Market Square in Ourtown, Nebraska.

All of the autos, freshly polished and proudly shown off by their owners, are rare and valuable relics from a bygone era. Included in the exhibit will be a black Luxury Lance once driven in President Politico's inaugural parade, along with a one-of-a-kind Palomino Motor Car.

-more-

Cars

2

    The gathering will be a unique opportunity to see and hear a bit of the country's past. According to organizer Albert Auto, owner of Auto Car Restoration Inc., some of the automobiles have been preserved, while others have been meticulously restored to their original condition. Mr. Auto estimates that as many as 1,000 people will stop by Market Square between 10 a.m. and 5 p.m. to rekindle old memories.

    For more information, contact Albert Auto at (555) 555-2222, or visit the Web site, autocarrestoration.com.

-end-

(b) The information is not pertinent to that medium's audience. Sometimes this can be difficult to judge, but just remember that all publications and broadcasts are aimed toward some particular group of people, and it is up to the editor or producer to decide whether or not your announcement will be of interest to them.

(c) The copy would require too much rewriting. To avoid this problem, follow the rules for appearance and format. With the volume of mail received by the media, time is not available to rewrite an incorrectly prepared release.

(d) The event is located too far away for convenient coverage. Don't send invitations to activities that aren't in a particular newspaper's circulation area or a TV station's viewing area, for example.

(e) Your news release is mistaken for junk mail. This can be caused by a mistake as simple as a badly-worded subject line in your e-mail. Or, if your message looks more like an advertisement than a news release, it can be thrown out at first glance.

(f) The press release is not typed on letterhead. If you don't have business letterhead, design some before you begin your publicity program. Your enterprise must have the legitimacy that comes from professional-looking letterhead.

(g) The statement is too long and rambles on for pages. All that is *truly* necessary in a news release are the four Ws: who, what, where, and when. If the recipients want more information, they will contact you and ask for it. That's why you include your telephone numbers and e-mail address.

2. Fate number two: Being put on hold

Not seeing your news immediately does not necessarily mean that your publicity attempt has fallen flat. Occasionally the media hold onto a press release with the idea of doing a major article on the subject in the future.

This can happen because your particular industry is expected to make headlines soon, because a magazine is planning a future issue on a topic like yours, or even because the media like to keep some "space-fillers" for emergencies. So don't despair. The possibility for publicity always exists as long as you are actively sending out notices.

3. Fate number three: Becoming a one-liner

A frequent result of publicity attempts in the print media is having a full-page press release shortened to one sentence, no matter how well prepared. But considering the potential audience, being mentioned at all is a worthwhile achievement.

Remember, every time your name appears in print, people will see it and remember it. And each time one of your press releases is chosen for publication, you build credibility with the media.

4. Fate number four: As is

In some cases your press releases will be received by the media and published or broadcast in full, just as you typed them. When that happens, you'll know you have succeeded not only in selecting a newsworthy topic, but also in writing your release in the best possible form. Although it might seem that every press release deserves this type of treatment, such an achievement is actually quite rare due to the stiff competition for free media attention.

5. Fate number five: Making the big time

The best possible result in any publicity attempt is being singled out for a flattering feature story. When that happens, the media will call and let you know that there is interest in expanding on your release and either proceed with questions over the telephone or set up an interview to be held later.

h. TO PHONE OR NOT TO PHONE

In all cases, once you send a press release, it's up to you to determine whether or not it was used by the media. Never call the media to ask when it appeared or why it was ignored. Members of the media are willing to give free coverage to those announcements they consider worthwhile, but don't ask journalists to become your personal clipping and consulting service. So each time you mail a press release, make a point of checking carefully for its publication or broadcast. And if you think you might miss seeing or hearing an announcement, ask employees, friends, relatives, or members of your organization to help by letting you know whenever they notice your name in the media.

i. ADD TO YOUR PUBLICITY PLANNER

It's important, as time goes on, that you maintain a permanent file of all the press releases you send. That way you'll always have a record in case the media ever call with a question. And always print out your electronic news releases, so you'll have a permenant record of them.

So take a moment now and label a new file folder in your Publicity Planner "Press releases sent." And whenever you prepare a press release, always make one extra copy for yourself.

Store your press releases in chronological order with the most up-to-date release at the front and the oldest at the back. Refer to them whenever you need a guide to follow.

Many groups that sponsor annual events actually send a similar news release every year by simply following the examples they have saved.

This can be especially helpful in situations where the publicity chairperson changes from year to year. Such permanent records will provide continuity to the program.

6
PREPARING PUBLICITY MATERIALS: PHOTOGRAPHS AND ILLUSTRATIONS

a. INTRODUCTION

A printed page doesn't capture attention the way a photograph or a drawing does. That's why most publications on the newsstands use big, bright pictures to lure shoppers into buying.

You can use the same lure by adding photographs and diagrams to your press releases. Print editors often pay more attention to announcements that include an attractive illustration. And, should your press release be published, the accompanying picture will add both interest and prominence to your story.

Although every press release does not require a photograph, high quality pictures definitely improve your chances of being mentioned in print. In this chapter you will learn how illustrations can enhance your message, when to send photos along with your press releases,

Be sure to decide what you want to say about yourself or your company when selecting a picture.

what kinds of pictures to use, and how to package them. Instructions are also given for identifying the photos and for writing captions.

b. DECIDE ON YOUR OBJECTIVES

Photographs, sketches, and diagrams can play different roles in your presentation to the press. Some of the purposes they serve are —

- (a) to display your product,
- (b) to portray your place of business,
- (c) to mold your corporate image,
- (d) to familiarize readers with your face,
- (e) to depict a project that's not yet completed, and.
- (f) to illustrate statistics, as in a graph.

Before you decide to use a picture, consider your objectives. What image are you trying to convey of yourself or your organization? For example, if an article about a company is accompanied by a photograph showing a person in a chicken costume handing out plastic eggs to children, what kind of impression would you have of the company? Would you form a different opinion of the company if the picture showed a woman wearing a business suit and sitting behind a desk surrounded by shelves of law books? Before you send any illustrations, think about what you want them to "say."

c. WEIGH THE ADVANTAGES

Including an illustration with your press release gives you a distinct advantage over the competition for a number of reasons:

- (a) An eye-catching image can convince an editor to set your story apart from the others on a page, resulting in higher visibility for your announcement.
- (b) A photograph heightens the impact of a story, meaning that readers will tend to remember you longer.
- (c) By providing the media with an actual look at what is being promoted, you increase your chances of being singled out for a feature story.

d. WHEN ARE VISUALS APPROPRIATE?

Even though photographs can be a valuable asset in a publicity drive, they are not always necessary. Certainly, radio stations do not need your photos to prepare their broadcasts. And television stations would prefer to get their own video, when possible. Visuals are most appropriate for the print media, but even segments of the print media will set aside your photos and rely only on their own photographers.

Generally, the best method for determining when to send illustrations is to look at the actual publications to which you will be sending your notices. If, for example, your daily newspaper has a section of business announcements accompanied by photographs, you can assume that your picture has a good chance of being used. On the other hand, if the paper to which you're mailing your submission never runs photos, don't send one.

Some publications, such as college alumni magazines, almost always print the photographs sent, while others, like glossy magazines, usually print only pictures taken by their own photographers. But if you really want a definitive answer, don't hesitate to call and ask. You don't need to talk to the editor or the assistant editor. Just call the publication's office and ask whether they ever publish photos received with press releases. If the answer is yes, ask if there are any special requirements.

e. GUIDELINES

Like press releases, photographs and illustrations receive additional attention from the press if they have been prepared with care. Here are some tips to give your contributions a professional look.

For computer-based graphics or photos, you'll want to consider the file size and format. You might send a file that's easy to view, and advise the recipients that a high-resolution copy is available.

1. Size

For distribution to the print media, photographs are expected to be a standard size, measuring either five inches by seven inches, six by eight, or eight by ten. Sketches should conform to the same requirements.

Make sure you conform to the style of the publication to which you are submitting your photograph. For example, don't send a color photograph to a publication that is only printed in black and white.

2. Style

For publications that are printed only in black and white, the standard photograph is known as a "black-and-white glossy," which refers not only to the color, but to the preferred shiny finish as well. A matte finish is acceptable for drawings and other illustrations, which should also be black and white.

For publications printed in color, it is advisable to call and ask for requirements, because many editors will accept only color transparencies or slides.

3. Composition

For best results, always send pictures that have a clear, sharp image. Since photographs will occasionally be trimmed to fit on a page, you should never pose with your hands (or props) on or near your face. That way, if the picture is cropped close to your face, no extraneous shadows or images will interfere with the portrait. Make sure your background doesn't make it appear as if things are "growing" out of your head, like TV antennas, lamps, or flagpoles.

4. Labelling

Always put a label on your photographs or illustrations for easy identification by the media, always making sure the label doesn't interfere with the visual itself. Include the full names and titles of everyone shown, being careful to state specifically which individual is where in the picture. It is also helpful to include the name of the organization. Type the information on a plain label or piece of paper and tape it to the back of the picture.

5. Captions

A caption is not the same as a label. Whereas a label is just a list of names, a caption is a sentence or a paragraph describing the action shown in the photograph. While every picture or drawing *must* have a label, captions are not required because most publications have people on staff to write them.

If you would like to include a caption, also referred to as a cut line, to a hard copy of your photo, simply type a few explanatory sentences onto white paper, tape it to the bottom of the picture, and fold it back. Captions to electronic visuals should likewise be separate from the visual itself. As a guide when writing captions, try to include the "Four Ws": who, what, when, and where. Sample 8 illustrates the difference between labels and captions.

6.   Especially for photographs

Regardless of the topic of the story, there is one photograph that is always acceptable to the print media: the "head shot." A head shot is a head-and-shoulders studio portrait similar to those in every high school and college yearbook. It is almost always appropriate to submit such a photograph of the person most closely associated with the organization being publicized. Other suitable poses depend on the activity involved. A group photograph, an action shot, a view of your shop, a picture of your product, or even a photograph of a drawing are all acceptable, as long as the other basic guidelines are met.

7.   For diagrams only

Occasionally an item or event is better represented by a diagram than a photograph. This type of illustration can range from a simple pen-and-ink sketch to a complex statistical graph.

If you opt for a drawing, be sure to send a professional-looking product. A photocopy or scanned image is fine as long as it is clear. To achieve this, begin with a perfect original and photocopy it using only the finest equipment. A copy must be as sharp as an original or the publication won't use it.

8.   Mailing

Never fold your illustrative material. Wrinkled pictures will not be used. Whenever you send photos or drawings, reinforce the mailing envelope with cardboard or enclose the press release and the picture in a stiff folder.

And don't expect to receive your pictures back, because the rule at most media outlets is that photographs submitted with press releases are not returned to sender. Not only do newspapers and magazines lack the staff to return photographs, many want to keep the pictures on file for possible re-use with future articles.

f.   SOURCES

It's not mandatory to pay a photographer or hire a graphic artist to get a picture in the paper. You can take your own photos or create your own illustrations as long as the results are of a high quality.

SAMPLE 8
LABELLING AND CAPTIONING FOR PHOTOGRAPHS

1. Label: Tana Fletcher, co-author of *Getting Publicity*

Caption: Journalist and lecturer Tana Fletcher has announced the new edition of her book, *Getting Publicity*, co-authored with television newswoman Julia Rockler. An invaluable guide for those wishing to gain free publicity, the book is published by Self-Counsel Press and is available at bookstores throughout North America.

2. Label: Tom Talker (left), owner of Talk of the Town Telephone Store, presenting trophy to Bill Business, winner of the 20— Talk of the Town Tennis Tourney.

Caption: Bill Business won this year's Talk of the Town Tennis Tourney, held in April to raise money for the Hometown Children's Organization. Mr. Business, shown here on the right, accepted the trophy from Tom Talker, sponsor of the event and owner of the Talk of the Town Telephone Store.

3. Label: Katy Cook, Campette Scout

Caption: The Campette Scouts of Anyvillage, Alberta, have announced their annual bake sale, to be held Saturday, September 15, 20— at the Anyvillage Elementary School from 10 a.m. to 2 p.m. Organized to raise money for a camp van, the sale will include hundreds of items prepared with special low-fat, low-calorie ingredients, such as the "Bountiful Bran" muffins shown here by Campette Scout Katy Cook.

4. Label: Betsy's Best Bottle Dryer, manufactured by Betsy's Best Co. of Troutfishing, Colorado

Caption: Betsy's Best Co. of Troutfishing, Colorado, has introduced Betsy's Best Bottle Dryer. Priced at $19.95, it works instantly on any size bottle by forcing air through a lightweight plastic pump. It is available at hardware stores everywhere.

If you are seeking outside help, however, try these sources:

(a) Call your local newspapers, both large and small, and ask the individual photographers or graphics specialists about working for you on a freelance basis.

(b) Look in the Yellow Pages under "Photographers" for any who specialize in publicity photos.

(c) Check the Yellow Pages for "Graphic Designers" to help with illustrations.

(d) Find out if there are any talented amateur photographers or artists among the members of your clubs or organizations.

g. ADD TO YOUR PUBLICITY PLANNER

When you are ready to begin your publicity program, collect photographs suitable for enclosing with your press releases. Prepare for this now by labelling a folder in your Publicity Planner "Publicity Photos." Then, any time you get a photograph you think might be suitable for sending, file it for future consideration. Save a printout of all your computer visuals as well as a back-up of those files for safekeeping. If you take your own pictures, you might also keep an envelope of negatives for those pictures you plan to use again. If you pay a professional photographer, order as many copies of the photos as you think you might need at one time and keep them handy in the same folder.

If you need a photographer or graphic designer to help you with your images, consult the Yellow Pages, local newspapers, or the members of your clubs and organizations.

The frequency with which you send photos is strictly a personal decision. One woman, who launched a publicity campaign with the express purpose of making a name for herself as an independent consultant, had 200 photos printed at a time. Another woman, who was attempting to carve out a career as a professional lecturer, managed to make three photographs last for an entire year. A third woman, a novelist, has a new picture taken every time she wants to enclose one with a press release.

In every case it's wise to re-examine your photos from time to time and make sure they're not outdated. Before you mail any illustrations, use Checklist 2 to analyze their appropriateness and review your preparation.

CHECKLIST 2
REVIEW YOUR PHOTOGRAPHS AND DRAWINGS

1. In considering whether or not to include a photograph or diagram along with your press release, ask yourself how an illustration would enhance your message.

   Does the publication use photographs and drawings?

   _____Yes   _____No

   Does the picture display your product to advantage?

   _____Yes   _____No

   Does the illustration make your point clearer?

   _____Yes   _____No

   Does the photograph project the correct image?

   _____Yes   _____No

2. In the picture or drawing:

   Is your attention drawn to the desired subject?

   _____Yes   _____No

   Does the subject fill the frame?

   _____Yes   _____No

   Is the image clear and well-focused?

   _____Yes   _____No

   If it's a reproduction, is it as sharp as the original?

   _____Yes   _____No

3. When sending photographs and diagrams:

   Is each picture clearly labelled?

   _____Yes   _____No

   Do any of the illustrations require a caption to clarify the scene?

   _____Yes   _____No

   Are the photographs and diagrams properly protected with cardboard for mailing?

   _____Yes   _____No

7
MAKING THE MOST OF A MEDIA KIT

a. INTRODUCTION

For most of your publicity attempts, you will simply be sending a press release to the media, sometimes with a photograph. But occasionally — when you are sponsoring a major event or have won a particularly prestigious award, for example — there are going to be times when you want to offer a more detailed presentation to the media. This may be no more than once or twice a year, but for those times you can mail out a more complete package of information called a media kit. This kit includes not only a press release and a photograph, but also a few other carefully chosen items that are described in this chapter.

The media kit, or press kit as it is also known, is one of the most valuable components in any successful publicity program. Made up of an inexpensive two-pocket paper folder filled with a few informational items relating to your organization, it can be the most effective weapon in your publicity arsenal. And whether you mail it to the media like a press release or carry it with you to give to reporters at events that receive press coverage, it can prove to be the key that unlocks the door to media access.

In this chapter, you will learn how to assemble a media kit for use in your own publicity program. There is a thorough discussion of the items to include as well as an explanation of the purpose and objectives of a media kit.

In the next chapter, you will find further instructions for creating a specialized "new product release" media kit for use whenever you are introducing a new product or service for the first time.

b. THE ROLE OF A MEDIA KIT

In a drive for public attention, the role of a media kit is similar to that of a good will ambassador: an envoy sent forth to promote a positive impression of an enterprise. When you prepare a media kit, you will be gathering into one folder an assortment of materials that portray you or your organization in such an interesting, informative, and professional manner that the recipient will feel compelled to grant you media coverage.

Carefully compiled to depict a specific image, the media kit allows you to put your best foot forward when meeting the media. Among its many uses, it can —

(a) be sent to members of the media to introduce yourself or your organization,

(b) announce a major event such as a convention, an exhibition, or a grand opening,

(c) be mailed to the producers of radio and television shows to suggest yourself as an interview subject or talk-show guest,

(d) supplement an interview the media has already requested,

(e) invite the media to attend a paid event or gathering by including complimentary press passes,

(f) be carried with you to meetings, exhibitions, and gatherings where members of the press might be present, and

(g) proclaim the official beginning — or the successful completion — of any long-term public project, from a charitable fund-raiser to a new recreation center.

Your media kit should act as a good will ambassador, giving the media a positive impression of you and your enterprise.

Whenever the opportunity arises, you may offer a media kit to journalists — not to ballyhoo your business, but as an aid in preparing their stories. In fact, once you decide what to put into your own media kit, it's a good idea to always have at least two copies in case an opportunity for publicity presents itself. Keep some at your office, carry two in your briefcase, have a few at home, and take several along to conventions, conferences, and other meetings.

Wherever there might be members of the media in attendance, you should have your media kit available. Even if you are participating in a group activity with hundreds of other participants, having a personalized media kit will allow you to single yourself out to the media. Think of your media kit as your publicity business card. Don't go anywhere without it.

c. PREPARE THE COVER

The first step in putting together your media kit is to purchase the cover. The most practical and popular choice is a folder, made of cardboard or heavy paper, with two inside pockets. Slightly larger than standard typing paper, these folders are available in a choice of colors. Quite inexpensive, they are available in office supply stores and catalogues, as well as most places that sell school supplies.

When choosing the cover for your media kit, it's not necessary to spend extra money on glittery styles because the media looks for substance, not shine. But if your business has a particular color with which it is associated, you might want to choose that shade for your kit.

If you plan to use a lot of media kits, you can order custom-printed covers with your logo and the name of your organization on the front. Otherwise, you do need to identify the outside of your press kit by applying stick-on address or mailing labels.

If you have no personalized, pre-printed labels, simply type the name and address of your organization on a blank label and press it onto the cover.

d. CONTENTS

In content, media kits are as varied as the organizations seeking publicity because each one is unique — a customized presentation. In putting together your own packet, you will be free to include any

Think of your media kit as your publicity business card — don't go anywhere without it.

elements you believe will show off your business, yourself, or your association to best advantage. But avoid making your presentation look like a commercial; never include any of your advertisements.

Among the materials considered standard in media kits are a press release, a photograph, a brochure, a business card, a cover letter, and several specially prepared handouts (a fact sheet, a biography, a list of questions) that are fully explained below.

Following is a list of the inserts to consider when assembling your own media kit. Please note that nothing handwritten should be included. Everything must be typed neatly and accurately in standard typeface and black ink, although only the press releases need to be double spaced to allow room for editors' marks.

1. Business card

When you are assembling a media kit, always begin with a business card. Most of the folders you will find in stores even have a pre-cut slot in one of the pockets for displaying your card. If not, you can staple a business card to the pocket so that it shows as soon as the folder is opened.

2. Press release

The media kit itself is fairly generic and suitable for any number of different occasions. A press release serves to give your media kit the focus it needs. If you are using the media kit to announce several different achievements or activities at the same time, you can even include more than one press release in a single kit.

See Sample 9 for an example of a press release to accompany a media kit.

3. Cover letter

A cover letter, or letter of explanation, should always be included in a media kit. Written using standard business letter format, it should be addressed personally to the individual to whom you are sending it. However, if you are preparing an especially large number of kits and don't have the time to type a personal address on every cover letter, the salutation, "Dear Member of the Media" is acceptable. Whenever possible, though, address each letter to the actual recipient.

CAMPETTE SCOUTS

POST OFFICE BOX AAA
ANYVILLAGE, ALBERTA Z1P 0G0
Telephone: (555) 555-5555
Fax: (555) 555-1111
E-mail: ccamper@campettescouts.org

PRESS RELEASE

September 1, 20—
For Immediate Release

Contact: Constance Camper
Daytime: (555) 555-5555
Evening: (555) 555-1212
E-mail: ccamper@campettescouts.org

Fundraiser to Focus on Flavor with Fewer Calories

Reduced-calorie cookies and cakes will be sold at the Anyvillage Campette Scouts' annual bake sale, Saturday, September 15, 20—, at Anyvillage Elementary School from 10 a.m. to 2 p.m.

Planned to raise money for a new camp van, the sale will include hundreds of items, all made with special low-fat, low-calorie ingredients.

"This is one bake sale everyone can enjoy without feeling guilty," says regional Campette Leader Constance Camper.

Campette Scouts, an international organization founded in 1939, sponsors summer camp outings for thousands of five- to fifteen-year-old girls each year. A nonprofit group, Campettes depend on donations to fund all their activities each year.

For further information, call (555) 555-5555 or visit the Campette Scouts Web site at campettescouts.org.

-end-

A cover letter is more personal than a press release — it is a one-to-one communication between you and the recipient.

The content of the cover letter differs markedly from that of the press release because the cover letter is personal — a one-to-one communication between you and the recipient. Where a press release contains information intended for the public, the details in a cover letter are meant strictly for the media.

An example of this would be a media kit announcing a three-day home furnishings exhibit being held in your city's convention center. While the press release might mention that the public is invited, admission is free, and the hours are from nine to five, the cover letter would advise the media that there has been a room set aside for media members to use as a lounge.

Or, in a media kit introducing a new business, the press release might mention the location and the service available, while the cover letter could offer extra photographs to the media upon request.

Cover letters vary according to the purpose of the press kit and the individual to whom they're sent. But in most cases they begin by introducing the sender and end with an offer of further assistance.

In writing your own cover letters, follow these general guidelines and you'll boost your success rate:

(a) Use business letterhead.

(b) Be cordial in your tone, not confrontational.

(c) Compliment the recipient's publication or program.

(d) Explain briefly the reason you are sending the media kit, beginning with one particularly significant statement, such as "This year, the Anycity Business Women's Business Club is celebrating its fourth anniversary."

(e) Mention the availability of any graphics or visuals you didn't include in the kit, such as color slides or videotape. (Only professional quality video should be offered.)

(f) Explain that you are available to answer any questions, but never *demand* coverage.

See Sample 10 for an example of a cover letter.

4. Visuals

When sending a press kit to the *print* media, it pays to include one or more high quality pictures because those kits with attractive photos are often chosen to be featured prominently. If you have such extras

CAMPETTE SCOUTS

POST OFFICE BOX AAA
ANYVILLAGE, ALBERTA Z1P 0G0
Telephone: (555) 555-5555
Fax: (555) 555-1111
E-mail: ccamper@campettescouts.org

September 1, 20—

Dear Channel 1 Assignment Editor:

In this era of health-conscious consumerism, even the old-fashioned bake sale has been revised. Our annual Campette Scout fundraiser will, for the first time, feature recipes chosen for their dietary content as well as flavor. This was an idea of a local Campette member and has generated the support of one of our local health associations (see letter enclosed in media kit).

This might make an interesting item for your weekly nutrition segment on the 5 p.m. news. Whatever your focus, the Campette Scouts hope you'll be able to include coverage of our event on your busy schedule. Scout leaders and members — including the 14-year-old Campette who suggested the healthy entries — will be available for interviews or any information you might need.

We've set aside press parking at the bazaar. Just look for the spaces marked "Administration."

Please contact me if I can be of any other assistance.

Sincerely,

Constance Camper, Region II Leader

as color slides or transparencies, mention their availability in the cover letter rather than sending them in the kit. Simply write, "Color slides are available upon request."

Although television is much less likely to use photographs, illustrations will still serve to enhance your media kit by making your story more visually exciting and bringing it to life for the reader. In addition, if you are being considered as an interview subject for TV, the recipient will be happy to have a preview of what you look like.

If you have any professional video available, describe the subject matter, the length, and the format. Generally, television professionals avoid VHS tapes and accept only the professional broadcast formats.

5. Fact sheet

One item included in many media kits is a page called a "fact sheet." Typed on business stationery and headlined with the words FACT SHEET (approximately two lines below the letterhead, all in capital letters), its purpose is to provide the media with instant research data on the history and significance of the subject of the kit.

A fact sheet is intended to list a firm's milestones and accomplishments in concrete terms, but is flexible enough to include different information for different situations. Where one firm's fact sheet might mention the civic contributions of company executives, another's might address production and sales statistics.

Regardless of the type of endeavor being promoted, the fact sheet should always highlight the most positive aspects of an endeavor while remaining accurate and informative. See Sample 11 for a sample fact sheet.

6. Biography

Another element frequently seen in media kits is a page pertaining to the background of the owner, founder, president, or leader of the company or organization. With nonprofit groups and other associations, this page is sometimes omitted, although a biography of the founder, current president, or person being honored is considered appropriate.

In a biography it's not necessary to state every fact about someone's life, just those that best demonstrate an individual's accomplishments, such as education, awards, professional experience, and other achievements. Personal information, including place of birth

CAMPETTE SCOUTS

POST OFFICE BOX AAA
ANYVILLAGE, ALBERTA Z1P 0G0
Telephone: (555) 555-5555
Fax: (555) 555-1111
E-mail: ccamper@campettescouts.org

FACT SHEET

HISTORY: Founded in 1959 by Olga Outdoors, Campette Scouts is an international organization dedicated to sponsoring summer camping vacations for girls aged five to fifteen.

FOUNDER: The first Campette Scout chapter was formed by 16 girls, ages 11 to 15, who organized campfire outings in their hometown of Anywhere, Alberta.

GROWTH: By 1985, the Campette Scouts had encircled the globe with more than 783 chapters in 13 nations.

OUTSTANDING ALUMNI: The Campette Scouts are proud of their distinguished alumni, including First Lady Wendy Writer and United Nations Ambassador Roberta Representative.

TODAY: There are more than 70,000 current members of Campette Scouts. A total of 912 chapters are active in 15 countries.

Keep clippings of any articles in which you have been mentioned, along with any work you have had published, in your media kit.

and other members of the family, may be listed if pertinent, but is not required.

The biography should be typed on business stationery bearing the name of the organization and headed BIOGRAPHY, typed in all capital letters approximately two lines below the letterhead. See Sample 12 for a guide to the style of a biography.

7. Clippings and quotes

If you or your organization have ever been mentioned in a magazine or newspaper story, include copies of the articles in your media kit. To create the best impression, cut out the original article and paste it to a piece of plain white paper. Then clip the title and date from the same publication and paste it neatly above the article. Photocopy this page for an easy-to-read and "custom-made" clipping.

Even if you were mentioned only briefly in print, or if you were talked about on radio or TV, you can still make use of such references in your press kit. You might place several quotes on one page, or you could merely list the media outlets where your name has appeared. For an example of how this is done, see Sample 13.

8. Examples of your own writing

If you have ever had any articles published, make copies and enclose them in your media kit as well. Use the same technique for photocopying as described for "Clippings and quotes" above. Save them in a folder you've marked "Published writing."

If you've never had any articles published but would like to, turn to chapter 14, "Writing as a Publicity Tool," for complete instructions.

9. Suggested questions

Because members of the media don't always have the time to conduct in-depth research before interviewing a subject, many press kits include a page of sample questions to serve as a guide for the interviewer. Although interviewers might not use the actual queries provided, such questions do help to clarify the subject matter.

Begin by typing SUGGESTED QUESTIONS as a heading, two lines below the letterhead on your business stationery. To make the sample questions meaningful, ask yourself the main points you'd like to make about your project. Include four to six questions, evenly spaced and centered on the page. See Sample 14 for an example.

CAMPETTE SCOUTS

POST OFFICE BOX AAA
ANYVILLAGE, ALBERTA Z1P 0G0
Telephone: (555) 555-5555
Fax: (555) 555-1111
E-mail: ccamper@campettescouts.org

BIOGRAPHY

Born in 1935 in the small community of Towne in northwest Canada, Olga Outdoors spent her childhood summers at a family cabin by Lake Loch.

She graduated from the Towne School in 1952 and received a bachelor's degree in English literature from All-National University in 1956.

Ms. Outdoors founded the first chapter of Campette Scouts in 1959 with her daughter and 15 classmates as members. The first meetings were at the Lake Loch cabin.

In 1998, Olga Outdoors was named "Outstanding Organizer" by the International League of Youth Activities for her work with the Campette Scouts.

Ms. Outdoors and her husband, Oscar, have three children and ten grandchildren. The couple lives in Towne and sponsors annual Campette Leader retreats at the old family cabin near Lake Loch.

CAMPETTE SCOUTS

POST OFFICE BOX AAA

ANYVILLAGE, ALBERTA Z1P 0G0

Telephone: (555) 555-5555

Fax: (555) 555-1111

E-mail: ccamper@campettescouts.org

Here is what the media have said about Campette Scouts:

"A praiseworthy organization." — *Anyvillage Gazette*

"Provides constructive summer instruction and fun to hundreds of youngsters." — *Anyvillage Channel 7 News*

"A worthwhile organization that deserves public donations of time and money." — *Anyvillage Magazine*

CAMPETTE SCOUTS

POST OFFICE BOX AAA

ANYVILLAGE, ALBERTA Z1P 0G0

Telephone: (555) 555-5555

Fax: (555) 555-1111

E-mail: ccamper@campettescouts.org

SUGGESTED QUESTIONS

1. Has Campette Scouts changed its mission over the years?

2. What kinds of things are communities doing to show their support for the Campette Scouts?

3. How are the funds spent?

4. Why should youngsters join the Campette Scouts?

5. How much does it cost to send a child to camp?

6. Why are the Campettes featuring low-calorie cookies in their bake sale?

10. Rolodex card

One of the most popular items in a press kit is a pre-printed Rolodex card for the recipient's telephone index. The media is very dependent on sources and by providing a Rolodex card with your name, address, telephone number, fax, e-mail address, and your specialty, you make yourself available as a future interview subject.

If you don't already have personalized Rolodex cards, it will probably pay you to have them made up, because they're also useful to hand out to your clients.

There's a trick to making your Rolodex card stand out from the rest, though. First, order the style with an index tab. Then, instead of printing your last name or the name of your company on the tab, print the *type* of service you sell or the product you offer.

For example, if your company is called Apple Tree Secretarial Service, you should have the words "Secretarial Service" printed on the index tab, not "Apple Tree."

That way, when a reporter needs to interview someone for a story about secretarial services, he or she will notice your card immediately.

Similarly, if your company is called Jones Accountants, you should have the tab on your Rolodex card imprinted with the word "Accountant" for easy reference. Even if your firm is called Pete's Plumbing, have the word "Plumber" printed on the tab, rather than "Pete's," because it tells your story in one word.

But if you don't have any extra money in your budget to have cards printed, don't worry. You can type the information yourself — like the man who owned a home-improvement company. But he didn't stop with one card in each press kit. Instead, he included six cards in every kit, each one with a different tab heading, including "Home Repair," "Plumbing," "Carpentry," and "Guttering." It proved to be worth the effort, though, when his homemade media kit resulted in no fewer than 20 articles, 25 radio interviews, and 2 television appearances.

11. Brochure

If your organization has an informative brochure, be sure to include a copy of it in your press kit.

Or, if the event you're publicizing has any promotional literature, enclose that in your kit as well.

12. Press passes

Whenever you send a media kit to announce a big event, whether it's a seminar, a convention, an exhibit, or any other important gathering, you should always invite the media to attend. You can do this in one of three ways, depending on your preference and the cost of the event.

(a) Cover letter

Use the cover letter to invite the media. Always mention any special arrangements you have made for members of the press, such as a meeting room set aside for their use or a special interview opportunity you have arranged, along with any information they might need to get in the door. If you want to limit their numbers, just state, "We would like to invite up to four members of your staff to attend...."

(b) Require reservations

If you need to know exactly how many members of the media will be present, simply add a request that they respond only if they plan to attend. Provide a telephone number for the media to call and reserve space. Include a statement such as, "Free passes for the working press will be held at the door. Please phone (555) 555-5555 to register the names of those who will be attending."

(c) Send complimentary tickets

Include complimentary tickets in the media kit. There are no guarantees that the media will be interested in your undertaking, but you can help ensure coverage by sending at least two tickets — one for a reporter and one for a photographer.

e. DECIDE ON YOUR IMAGE

Before you actually put together your press kit, think about the impression you are hoping to make. Do you want your enterprise to appear to be small and friendly or large and complex? Is your desired image casual or formal, eccentric or businesslike? With a clear picture of your objective, your final presentation will be more effective.

The previous list of press kit components is not meant to be complete. On the contrary, it represents merely a beginning, a starting point from which to launch your own concept. The actual finished product depends completely on the image you wish to project of your

Whenever you send a media kit to announce a big event, be sure to invite the media to attend.

endeavor, your goals, and even your style. Before you go any further, stop and think for a moment about preparing a presentation for your own enterprise. Some other items you might want to send include —

(a) a list of your organization's achievements,

(b) a catalogue of your products,

(c) a graph showing the distribution of your funds,

(d) a chart demonstrating the need for contributions,

(e) copies of complimentary letters you have received, or

(f) clippings of articles showing the importance of your industry in today's economy.

As you assemble your press kit, be creative. Mix and match your materials to suit yourself as well as your intended targets. The media kit is the only part of your enterprise that many journalists will ever see. Make the most of your opportunity by sending the very best product you can.

f. SWEET STORIES OF SUCCESS

The most successful press kits are those that result in major media exposure for the sender. The following examples of real-life success stories should inspire you and give you additional ideas for using your imagination in creating your own press kit.

In one case, an innkeeper mailed his media kit to a national magazine, hoping to have his inn featured. Of course he included information about his own lodge, along with a few pictures. But as an added enticement he also sent colorful brochures highlighting several other tourist attractions in his town. The possibility for interesting background photos was all it took to convince an editor to send a reporter and photographer and to publish an article about the inn.

In another situation, a builder who was planning a residential development for senior citizens sent a press kit filled with elaborate drawings of the completed structure and a detailed list of the planned amenities. Even though the actual construction site was nothing but a pile of dirt at the time, the project received positive coverage in several newspapers, generating interest from potential tenants.

And in yet another scenario, a first-time novelist discovered that her publisher was unwilling to spend any money on publicity so she arranged her own promotion by calling a bookstore and offering to sign copies of her book in the store window. She sent a news release beforehand, and when a reporter showed up, the novelist was ready with a press kit she had prepared just for the occasion. As a result of her personal efforts, the fledgling author was featured not only in the local paper, but also in a magazine article written by the same reporter.

The moral is that journalists are always looking for an interesting story. And an attention-getting media kit can be exactly what you need to become that story.

g. ADD TO YOUR PUBLICITY PLANNER

A well-organized Publicity Planner should make it easy for you to put together a media kit, even at a moment's notice. You should be able to assemble an informative packet by merely reaching for a media kit cover folder and filling it with items from your publicity planner files.

With this in mind, plan to have a file folder for each of the following categories, along with any others that seem especially well-suited to your own personal publicity program.

- Biography
- Brochures
- Business cards
- Catalogues
- Clippings and quotes
- Fact sheet
- Industry news
- Letters from happy customers
- Media kit folders
- Media kit labels
- Promotion ideas
- Publicity photos
- Published writing
- Rolodex cards

Journalists are always looking for an interesting story, and an attention-getting media kit can be exactly what you need to become that story.

- Stationery

- Suggested questions

Media kits are an important part of an overall publicity program, but you won't be expected to send them every time you seek media attention; it would be too expensive and too time-consuming. A press release is all that's needed for most announcements. But try to keep a few media kits handy, and do plan to send one every year to various media outlets. If you send more than one every six months to the same place, though, the impact will definitely be diminished.

8
ANNOUNCING A NEW PRODUCT

a. INTRODUCTION

Although the media kit is useful in any number of different circumstances, if you should ever have the occasion to introduce a brand new product, service, or business for the very first time, you can reap additional rewards by sending a specialized media kit known as a "new product release" media kit. Exactly the same in appearance and purpose as a standard media kit, the difference lies in its approach to the media.

By placing the emphasis — both in the cover letter and the press release — on the "first-time" or "introductory" aspect of the item being promoted, the sender can often gain special attention in the media.

As an example, two home improvement contractors once successfully launched their own do-it-yourself wallpapering video by sending out 3,000 "new product release" media kits at the same time to media outlets throughout North America. Within months, the free publicity their product received in newspapers and magazines created an enormous demand for the video.

In fact, whenever you see a story in the media about a newly released record album, a recently published book, or the latest in modern machinery, odds are that it's because a new product release kit was sent to the press.

New product release kits are popular with the media as a way to showcase the latest in lifestyle trends, and each submission receives consideration. But you can increase your own chances of being chosen for coverage by paying attention to how you assemble your information.

b. THE NEW PRODUCT RELEASE MEDIA KIT

Just as with any other media kit, the new product release media kit is made up of an inexpensive paper folder with two inside pockets into which you place a few carefully selected materials. The contents are similar to those of a standard media kit and include such items as a press release, a cover letter, a photograph, a descriptive brochure, and a business card.

There are two basic differences, however, between a standard media kit and a new product release media kit. First, a new product release media kit must be mailed to coincide with the initial availability of the product being featured. And, second, if the product being promoted is not too costly, an actual sample can be included in the new product release media kit. Typically, the products most often included are small items such as books, videotapes, and games.

When sending an actual product, if it isn't flat enough to fit into one of the pockets of the media kit folder, it should be fastened to the outside of the folder with a large rubber band or simply sent in the same mailing envelope with the media kit.

Also it's important to remember that hard-sell tactics are out of place in a new product release media kit. To achieve the best results, try to present your message from the consumer's point of view and your new product release media kit will invariably receive more favorable attention from the press.

For example, if you are a home builder and you are sending out a new product release media kit to introduce brand new "affordable"

A new product release media kit should coincide with the initial availability of the product being featured, and should contain a sample if possible.

housing, don't boast that you are the only builder who cares about consumers. Instead, use your press release to describe the benefits of your product *from the buyer's point of view.* In other words, rather than highlighting your own accomplishments with a statement like, "The Building Company is proud to be at the forefront in affordable housing," emphasize the benefits *for the consumer* by stating, "With only $6,000 cash, buyers can move right in as long as their total family income is at least $30,000 a year."

It is this consumer-oriented approach — making a special point of how a new product or service is beneficial to the public — that is the most important part of any new product release media kit. As a guideline, always be sure to ask yourself if your press release clearly describes how consumers will benefit from your product.

c. CONTENTS

The contents of a new product release kit is flexible, but ideally it will include the following components.

1. Press release

Every new product release kit requires a press release. In your press release, be sure to describe what it is that makes your offering unique and valuable — such as its size, shape, or capabilities. In addition, as with any press release, it is always appropriate to include a brief history, emphasizing anything of significance.

Personal or biographical information is not required; but it is important to include information about product availability, price, and purchase instructions. For a sample of a new product press release, see Sample 15.

2. Cover letter

A cover letter, while appropriate with a new product release, is not strictly required. If you choose to include a letter, offer your availability to answer any further questions. If you have special color photographs, slides, transparencies, or other visuals, mention their availability as well. See Sample 16 for a sample cover letter.

3. Photo

Depending on the size and price of your product, you can send the media either a picture or an actual sample. Since the media will keep

The most important part of any new product release media kit is explaining how the new product or service will benefit the consumer.

SAMPLE 15
PRESS RELEASE FOR NEW PRODUCT RELEASE KIT

BEST BOILERS
123 GOOD WAY
DANDYTOWN, IOWA 00000
Telephone: (555) 555-5555
Fax: (555) 555-1111
E-mail: bbest@bestboilers.com

PRESS RELEASE

September 1, 20—
For Immediate Release

Contact: Bob Best
Daytime: (555) 555-5555
Evening: (555) 555-6666
E-mail: bbest@bestboilers.com

Latest Technology Offers Hot Water in an Instant

Now every home owner can have hot water in an instant, thanks to Best Boilers' new faucet adapter, the Handy Hot.

The Handy Hot takes only minutes to install and saves water, time, and cooking energy every time it's used.

The portable adapter is about the size of a coffee mug and fits conveniently near any faucet, with little sacrifice of storage or counter space.

"It's like having a cup of tea within reach at all times," says Bob Best, president of Best Boilers. "And you never have to fill the kettle, or wait for it to boil," he adds.

Priced at $49.95, the Handy Hot is available at hardware stores from coast to coast. For further information, phone Best Boilers at (555) 555-5555.

-end-

BEST BOILERS
123 GOOD WAY
DANDYTOWN, IOWA 00000
Telephone: (555) 555-5555
Fax: (555) 555-1111
E-mail: bbest@bestboilers.com

September 1, 20–

Dear Member of the Media:

Best Boilers of Dandytown, Iowa, has recently introduced a brand new product, the Best Boiler Handy Hot Faucet Adapter, which allows any home owner to receive boiling water instantly from any faucet.

Until now, this type of installation was permanent and required a large investment of time and money. But now, with the Handy Hot, anyone can turn an ordinary tap into a super-heated spray within minutes.

Because I am convinced that consumers will want to know about this convenient new device, I am sending you a packet of information.

Please call me if you have any questions or if I can be of any help.

Sincerely,

Bob Best
President

If your business is service-based rather than product-based, you can create a product such a brochure filled with helpful hints about your service.

it, however, sending a sample is recommended only for inexpensive items. Some of the new products that individuals sometimes send include videotapes, books, brochures, packaged food products, and small items that fit inside media kit folders.

Whenever you choose *not* to send a sample of your product, however, try to include a photograph that clearly depicts the item you're promoting. Follow the guidelines for good publicity pictures, and do hire a professional photographer if necessary.

If you happen to be promoting a new service or even a community project, a photograph of you or your headquarters can be helpful.

4. Brochure

Include any informational brochures in the kit. If you have none, you can type a fact sheet to list any distinctive aspects of your offering. Follow the format for a standard media kit fact sheet, but focus on the product rather than an individual or a company.

d. CREATE A "PRODUCT" FOR A SERVICE-BASED BUSINESS

The purpose of a new product release kit is to enable you to place a product prominently in the media in order to create a demand for it. But you needn't miss out on such a worthwhile publicity opportunity simply because your own organization happens to be service-based.

Accountants, lawyers, consultants, paramedics, and any others involved in service-oriented professions can come up with an attention-getting "new product" of their own. With a little imagination, any type of enterprise can profit from a new product promotion.

Turn to Sample 17 for an example of how to write a new product release for a service-based business. Then note the following suggestions for preparing your own promotions.

1. Prepare a helpful hint brochure

One of the best ways for a service provider to produce a promotable "product" is by giving away a helpful brochure offering consumer advice. Even if you're not a writer, you can type out a list of the five or ten questions you hear most often from clients and provide a brief one- or two-sentence answer to each query.

WENDY WEDDINGTON, WEDDING CONSULTANT
4321 BRIDAL BOULEVARD
MYTOWN, BRITISH COLUMBIA Z1P 0G0
Telephone: (555) 555-5555
Fax: (555) 555-1111
E-mail: wweddington@email.com

PRESS RELEASE

March 1, 20—
For Immediate Release

Contact: Wendy Weddington
Daytime: (555) 555-5555
Evening: (555) 555-1212
E-mail: wweddington@email.com

Wedding Consultant Offers Free Consumer Hints

As the June brides-to-be prepare their trousseaux, many are asking the same questions: How far in advance must a bride select her gown? Who pays for what? Can a married woman be a bridesmaid? What kind of flowers are best?

Now the 25 most common wedding questions are answered in a new pamphlet, offered at no cost by bridal expert Wendy Weddington. "Any bride who knows the answers to these basic questions is well on her way to a wedding without worry," says Weddington.

To receive a free copy of Wendy Weddington's *Advice for Planning a Perfect Wedding*, send a legal-sized, self-addressed, stamped envelope to Wendy Weddington, Wedding Consultant, 4321 Bridal Boulevard, Mytown, British Columbia Z1P 0G0.

For further information, phone Wendy Weddington at (555) 555-5555 or e-mail her at wweddington@email.com.

-end-

The owner of a plumbing service, for instance, could offer a free list of maintenance tips; a landscape designer might prepare a set of simple instructions for tree-planting; a lawyer could provide advice about preparing wills; and an accountant might list ten tips for setting up a business.

These brochures can be very basic, but they should be professionally printed and feature your company's name, address, and telephone number. Your offering can be free or you can charge for it, but the media is always more receptive to no-cost offers of consumer help.

In preparing a new product release kit, always send the media a copy of any pamphlets or educational material you are offering to the public.

2. Give away a promotional item

Another way to create a "product" to stimulate interest in your service is by offering some type of promotional give-away. Depending on the nature of your enterprise, this might be anything from a free key chain imprinted with your company logo to your favorite family recipes.

In this case, when you prepare your press materials, send one of the promotional items along with the publicity packet.

3. Include information for ordering

Always include directions for ordering in your press release. You might say, "To order these helpful hints, simply send a self-addressed, stamped envelope to Henry Homeowner's Home Repair and Referral Service, 111 Home Street, Hometown, Montana 00000." Or, you could write, "This brochure is available at no cost by calling Wendy Weddington's Weddings, (555) 555-5555." For another example see Sample 15 earlier in the chapter.

e. FIND NEW PLACES TO SEND YOUR KITS

To locate the best places to send new product release kits, watch for opportunities whenever you read a magazine, watch television, or thumb through your daily paper.

In the print media, look for sections or columns specifically geared to featuring new offerings of products, services, shops, restaurants, clothing, and other items. Target any regular column showcasing subjects similar to yours.

In the broadcast media, you should watch and listen for references to specific new products, whether in a light vein, such as on a talk show, or in a straight news format.

Make a note of any programs that seem to be a suitable outlet to announce your product or service.

f. BE PREPARED TO FOLLOW UP

One caution regarding new product releases: always be ready to respond to consumer requests immediately and professionally in order to avoid complaints to the media that ran your release.

If the media is bothered with calls or letters from unhappy readers or viewers, you will immediately lose any future cooperation in your publicity efforts.

On the other hand, if the media should receive compliments about you following your new product release, you might be asked for a follow-up story, which will provide you with even more coverage.

g. ADD TO YOUR PUBLICITY PLANNER

To facilitate sending announcements of new products or services, label a folder "New product release."

Use it for filing items such as product specification sheets and other relevant data, any pamphlets you are offering to mail to consumers, and a copy of every new product press release you send.

9
SENDING OUT YOUR MESSAGE

a. INTRODUCTION

Before actually implementing your publicity campaign, it is crucial that you know where to send your announcements in order to generate coverage by the media. To accomplish this you will need to add one more element to your Publicity Planner — the media list.

The media list is a specialized mailing list. It includes the name, address, telephone number, program, contact people, and other pertinent data of every media target appropriate for your publicity efforts. Compiling and maintaining this list will streamline your publicity efforts and save time once you begin regular mailings.

In this chapter you will learn the four steps required for putting together a meaningful media list, for keeping it current, and for expanding it when necessary.

The four steps are —

(a) determining where and to whom to send press releases and media kits,

(b) preparing the mailing list,

(c) evaluating the results, and

(d) updating the list regularly.

First, label a new file folder in your Publicity Planner "Media list sources."

b. WHERE TO SEND YOUR INFORMATION

1. Broadcast media

Begin by analyzing the broadcast media — radio and television — for suitability as recipients of your press releases and other announcements. Although the needs of the two are not the same, both are vital to any media list.

(a) Television

Television provides a number of opportunities for publicity from the smallest local operation to the largest network. There are talk shows, news programs, variety hours, and even special-interest presentations.

Learn to watch television in a new way, focusing your attention on the kinds of shows where people like you are making contributions. Refer back to chapter 4, "Understanding Media Accessibility," and watch for the kinds of programs that might be available to you.

Watch the credits of the programs with pencil in hand to write down the name of the person you want to reach with your press releases. The following notes will help identify the correct contact person:

(a) In the case of news programs, you'll want to get the name of the assignment manager or assignment editor, if listed.

(b) For programs other than news, note the name of the producer. Do not send material to the executive producer, since that person is, by definition, removed from the day-to-day operations of the program.

Learn to watch television in a new way, focusing on the kinds of shows where people like you are making contributions. Watch the credits of these programs and write down the name of the person you want to reach with your press releases.

(c) To find the address of a television station, simply look up the station's call letters, such as ZXKY-TV, in your telephone directory.

Whenever you identify a television program that might be a possible publicity source, use Worksheet 4 as a guide for collecting the appropriate information about the program. You can make copies of the worksheet if you wish, and fill in the information on a separate sheet for each source you identify. Keep the information in the "Media list sources" file in your Publicity Planner.

(b) Radio

Whenever you have the opportunity, listen to interview programs on the radio and analyze them for publicity potential. When you hear a program that sounds promising for your publicity purposes, use a copy of Worksheet 4 to record the name of the station, the title of the show, and the types of subjects it covers. You can use your local telephone directory to get the station's address and telephone number. Call the station to find out who produces the show you're interested in, and to verify your information. Again, use Worksheet 4 to collect information about each radio program you think might be an appropriate target for your publicity efforts.

Once your media list is in place, it will be easy for you to send a press kit to a TV program or a radio station and suggest yourself as an interview subject. But you need to be familiar with the programs first.

2. Print media

In the print category you will be looking at every source of printed material that publishes announcements regarding social, business, and individual achievements and events. This category includes a wide variety of publications, such as magazines, newspapers, newsletters, alumni bulletins, club announcements, trade publications, and professional journals.

(a) Check your own mailbox

Begin by concentrating on the mail you receive each day. Look through it for any communiques which regularly carry announcements of individual accomplishments or scheduled events. Social

WORKSHEET 4
MEDIA LIST WORKSHEET

When you compile your media list, use this worksheet as a guide for the information you need to assemble.

1. Name of program, publication, wire service, or Web site:

   _____

2. If broadcast medium, name of station:

   _____

3. If print medium, name of column or section:

   _____

4. Title of contact person:

   _____

5. Name of contact person:

   _____

6. Mailing address, including station call letters:

   _____

7. Telephone numbers — general:

   _____

8. Telephone numbers — special departments:

   _____

9. Fax numbers:

   _____

10. E-mail:

    _____

11. Days, times, and frequency of publication or broadcast:

    _____

12. Deadline information:

    _____

13. Types of subjects covered:

    _____

14. Special requirements:

    _____

15. Dates information verified:

    _____

Check if: ☐ Print ☐ Radio ☐ TV ☐ Wire service ☐ Web site

clubs, neighborhood associations, civic organizations, religious centers, and educational institutions all send publications that might provide you with an opportunity for publicity.

Each time you discover a possible source, use a copy of Worksheet 4 as a guide for collecting the necessary information. From the publication's title page or list of staff members, write down the name, address, and telephone number of the publishing house or organization, and any other information you need.

In addition, save one or two pages from the publication showing announcements similar to those you plan to send. These will be useful as a reference when you prepare your own publicity material. Label them, and file them in the "Media list sources" folder.

(b) Newspapers

As you read your daily and weekly newspapers, spend a few extra minutes looking for sections where your press releases might fit. Be on the lookout for features that ask readers to send announcements of their own activities, such as community calendars and neighborhood reports. Frequently, at the end of such listings, are words like "Send information about your activities to...." Whenever you notice a likely recipient of your releases, copy the mailing information on a copy of Worksheet 4.

And don't overlook the writers who sometimes mention new products or trends in their regular columns. To write to these columnists, just address your news releases to them at the address of the publication given on the title page.

(c) Trade journals

No list of print media would be complete without the association and professional magazines known as "trade journals." From accounting to zoology, almost every occupation has its own publication today. And the good news for publicity seekers is that the editors are always seeking items of interest.

From now on, whenever you notice a trade-related periodical, pick it up and flip through the pages for columns highlighting announcements. Often these features have titles such as "People in the News" and carry photographs of the individuals mentioned. Once again, you can keep a sample for your file, but always record the name of the publication, the editor, and the mailing address.

(d) Magazines

Pay attention not only to the glossy national magazines, but also to the city, regional, and special-interest magazines. Notice those that mention new businesses, showcase new products, or spotlight new trends — not in the advertising pages, but in the articles and columns. Save any examples from magazines that might be suitable future outlets for your press releases. Use Worksheet 4 to prepare a sheet for each one listing the names of the editors that appear on the title page, the address, and any other pertinent data, such as deadline information.

(e) Entertainment guides

Many places offer tourists free or inexpensive guides listing local events, activities, and points of interest. Most often these publications are distributed where tourists congregate, including hotels, restaurants, and souvenir shops. Whenever you notice one, flip through it to see if you might take advantage of any opportunities for publicizing your company within its pages. If so, file a sample in your Publicity Planner for reference and record the mailing information.

(f) Miscellaneous

Begin to make it a practice to notice new or special-interest publications as possible targets for your press materials. Scan newsstands, pick up magazines in waiting rooms, and pay attention to what others are reading. By constantly being on the watch for possible media outlets, you can make your media list into a valuable asset.

3. News wire services

In many cases you will also want to send your press releases to the wire services in your area. Wire services are news-gathering organizations located throughout the world that provide information to other media including radio, television, and newspapers.

News wire services are staffed by reporters and editors who cover the events taking place in their own geographical area. Their stories are then instantly transmitted to other newsrooms.

News wire services provide an important service for other media. Small outlets with no reporters of their own, such as radio stations, depend on wire services for virtually all of their news. Major media players use the wire services as a kind of news "insurance" to make sure they don't miss any significant events around them.

In terms of the kinds of events covered, wire services generally mirror the metropolitan news media — major national news, local events, sports, and weather are all provided "on the wire."

Wire service reporters cover the major events in person, but for small business news or feature stories, the wire service staff is likely to get its information over the phone.

One of the main features of the news wire services is the daily log of events that will be covered in the news that day. This log is generally known as the "daybook." Its listings include a variety of activities from court cases to press conferences, trade shows, and award presentations. The daybook is so influential that for some news gathering agencies, the daily list of activities and events provides the main basis for assigning coverage each day.

The daybook listings themselves are fairly accessible to any news event that appears legitimate to the wire service staff. But receiving a one-line listing is not the same as actually getting media coverage, so even though you send a press release to your local news wire service, you will still have to contact all of your other target media as well.

To send your press releases to wire services, look in the telephone directory under "News Services." Call to find out which editor should receive your press release. Then keep a record of that information in your "Media list sources" file.

4. The World Wide Web

The Internet provides nearly unlimited possibilities but you'll want to target your electronic outreach as carefully as you do your other efforts. Use search engines to help identify the Web sites that will be most appropriate to contact with your information. Just as with other media, you'll notice that some Web sites are more receptive than others to input like yours.

5. Naming names in the media

Always try to reach the correct recipient with the press releases you send. Scoring a direct hit can save time and help you get your name in the news faster.

When addressing your material, it's an advantage to be able to target it directly to the person who decides its fate. In most cases you need only track down the person who holds the right job title, whether that's the assignment editor, producer, city editor, or other position.

It's always better to use the individual's actual name if you are confident that you have up-to-date information. But be warned: members of the media tend to move around frequently and you'll need to double check your contact names regularly — at least every six months. Don't be afraid to phone and ask.

If you would rather send your announcements to the person in charge of any particular department, the following list of titles should be helpful:

(a) Newspapers: (Fill in specific section, e.g., Business, Lifestyle, Calendar, etc.) Editor

(b) Magazines: (Fill in the name of the column, e.g., "New Products" or "Neighborly News") Editor

(c) Local television news: Assignment Editor, (Fill in name of TV station) Newsroom

(d) Television or radio talk show or variety program: Producer, (Fill in name of program)

(e) All-news radio: Assignment Desk, (Fill in name of station)

(f) Radio — other than all-news: News Desk, (Fill in name of station)

(g) Internet locations: carefully check over each site, to see what information they provide to contact them.

c. PREPARE A MEDIA LIST

Now that you have identified the places you might send your publicity materials, you are ready to assemble your actual mailing list. You will need to prepare and maintain it separately from any other mailing lists you might have.

First, decide which method will be most convenient. The following systems are the most widely used.

1. Rolodex

A Rolodex or a file box of index cards will provide the most flexibility for a media list by allowing you to remove or replace individual entries easily. In addition, the space on the cards provides a place for any personal notes or reminders.

2. Address book

An address book is more convenient to carry around than a card file, but frequent corrections and changes can render the entries difficult to read.

3. Separate sheets of paper

By using Worksheet 4 provided in this chapter, you can prepare a single sheet of information on every entry in your media list and file them in the "Media list sources" file in your Publicity Planner.

4. Computer

For some people a computer-generated list can be very functional, providing not only a method for updating, but also allowing you to print address labels automatically. If you are already using a similar system for your customer or membership mailing list, you might find it practical for your media mailing list as well.

5. Ready-made media lists

In addition to compiling a personalized media list, you can also obtain ready-made guides from a variety of sources.

(a) In many locales, a printed list of media outlets is available through business-related alliances such as the chamber of commerce, the board of trade, the convention and visitors bureau, and similar organizations.

(b) Most local publishers and broadcasters are listed in the telephone directory. You can create an instant list by simply copying the names and addresses directly out of the Yellow Pages.

(c) Call local governments for information. Many publish media lists and directories as a reference for new residents.

(d) Consult your local library. Most have at least one media directory available in the reference department.

(e) Use search engines to identify online media by region or category.

When sending out your news releases, remember to concentrate on the message, not the messenger. Just because you pay a small fortune to have your news release hand delivered, doesn't mean that it will reach the right person, or receive a better reception from that person.

d. GET THE INFORMATION OUT

You've written a sparkling news release. There's a compelling item of interest in it. You've identified the correct recipient — the person who can make it "happen." And now you're wondering how to draw extra attention to its arrival at its destination.

Should you send a private messenger, use an express delivery service, or even drive around from office to office delivering news releases yourself? The answer is no. Don't waste your time and money because the traditional mail service works just as well — as long as you allow a reasonable amount of time for delivery.

Regardless of how much you spend to send your announcements by way of costly delivery services, your news releases will only be delivered as far as the front desk. From there they will probably be put with the regular day's mail and not given any special attention at all. So once again, concentrate on the message, not the messenger.

1. To fax or not to fax

With the proliferation of fax technology has come small mountains of unwanted or "junk" faxes that, unfortunately for the sender, are often set aside or ignored by the media. There *are* appropriate times to send your message to a reporter or editor via fax, and then there are times when you'd be better off using the "old-fashioned" methods of communication.

(a) Fax advantages

The advantage of faxing your message, of course, is the immediacy. You might not have time to alert the media of an event happening on short notice, unless you make use of a fax. Your machine can report that the fax was received on the other end, so you have the assurance that the message went through.

(b) Fax drawbacks

Faxes are limited, though. If you're trying to convey urgency to the media, the fax may not be fast enough. Although faxes arrive quickly at their destination, there might not be anyone around to read them. If, for example, an airplane accidentally lands in the parking lot of your business and you want to alert the news media, a telephone call would be much more helpful than a fax.

And if your message isn't urgent, there's no reason to transmit by fax, because you lose the professional appearance and aesthetic appeal of your stationery. Fax paper is functional, but hardly official. And, of course, with a fax machine you're limited in what you send to the media. Your business or Rolodex cards cannot be faxed, for example.

(c) The right time to fax

As a general rule, when contacting the media think of fax technology as a supplement to other communication methods, not a replacement. When a reporter asks you for more information, for instance, a fax would be an ideal way of sending the details requested. However, you'll become a nuisance if you send unsolicited faxes and then make follow-up calls to see if they've arrived in good form.

Faxes are not the best way to make a first impression. When you're trying to show an image, your stationery is often much more impressive than a fax copy of your letterhead. Once you've established your identity, and your logo, for example, faxed corresponence becomes more acceptable.

2. Telephone facts

When you want publicity, avoid telephoning the media — at least under most circumstances. Members of the press are always working under deadline pressure with very little time to spare, and there is never enough staff to handle telephone inquiries.

One major metropolitan daily newspaper in the eastern United States recently reported receiving an average of nearly 20,000 individual pieces of mail and 7,000 fax pages in its newsroom *in a single day*. Imagine what would happen if all the people who corresponded in writing felt compelled to follow up with a phone call.

Plan to communicate by mail except in cases when your news is urgent — that is, it is taking place immediately or expected within the next 24 hours. If a truck filled with eggs should spill its contents outside your store and create a parking lot full of scrambled eggs, call the local media right away. If you have some genuine "breaking news," it deserves more timely attention than it will get by mail or fax, and there's a good chance you'll be the individual they interview. Of course, try not to overestimate the significance of your story, but never hesitate to call with a genuinely interesting occurrence or

Never call the media to ask if your press release has been used. Instead, keep track of where you send your releases and watch carefully to see if they appear.

newsworthy happening. On the other hand, don't call about an event that you've been planning for two weeks for which you never got around to sending press releases.

When you do call, the reporter might want to take the information directly over the telephone. But if he or she isn't willing to do so, you can offer to fax the information, which you will have to type up in press release form.

e.   EVALUATE AND UPDATE YOUR MEDIA LIST

Every time you send out press releases, you want to know where your announcement appeared and how much of it was used. Keep track of where you send your releases, and follow up by watching the next several issues of each publication for your announcement, listening to the radio, watching television, and going online to the targeted Web site. When people say they heard about you in the media, be sure to ask where they saw your notice. That way you'll be able to keep track of which media seem to be most receptive to your messages.

Never call the media to ask. Even if someone actually remembered receiving your communique from among the thousands that are sent, he or she would have no idea where or when it appeared. You can, however, search on the Internet for your clippings. Many newspapers, magazines, and other periodicals are available online, so you can check in both the current and archived records for mentions. Once you locate an article, print a copy to keep in your Publicity Planner.

If, after several attempts, your announcements are being ignored by one particular media outlet, attempt to remedy the situation. Try targeting a different person or a different department. But never contact the media and ask why your news releases aren't being used. Instead, consider the possibilities and make adjustments yourself.

For example, if you are mailing your press releases to the business editor but they aren't appearing in your local paper, see if they might fit into another section, such as the neighborhood report, and start sending them there instead. You might also try paying attention to the types of announcements that do get picked up by the media. Notice how they differ in content from your own and adjust your news releases to fit in with the others.

It's possible that your messages are merely arriving too late. To determine a deadline, contact the media outlet and ask what the deadline is for news releases in that particular section. Be sure to note the information in your media list.

Keep your media contact list up to date. Make sure that the places you send your press releases are still the same — that they're still carrying the same content, appearing at the same time, and are headed by the same individuals. Occasionally a change in ownership can mean a change in publication and broadcast policy as well. If you hear that a publication has gone out of business, remove the name from your list right away. Also, be on the lookout for new publications and add them to your list whenever possible. Maintaining a media contact list is an ongoing effort, but it is necessary to ensure that your publicity attempts will not be wasted.

f. ADD TO YOUR PUBLICITY PLANNER

Now you need to set up the system you will use for compiling your media list. If you should choose to use index cards, purchase the size you find most suitable. Be sure to buy a file box for storing them. If you get a container that closes securely, you'll find it's easier to carry with you because the cards will not fall out even if the box tips.

If you prefer a Rolodex, use the same criteria for selecting the style as when you purchase your Publicity Planner filing system. If, for example, you will be carrying it outdoors, buy one that closes. If you will have it on your desk top in plain view, choose one that looks different from the others on your desk so that you can tell at a glance whether it's the customer list or the media contact list.

For computer users, keep your media list in a separate file and, of course, make a back-up copy regularly.

Whenever you discover a possible new source for media publicity, turn to Worksheet 4 as a reference and assemble all the appropriate information. Store the data in your "Media list sources" file and add the source to your actual mailing list — whether it's a card file or a computer list.

10
MASTERING THE MEDIA INTERVIEW

a. INTRODUCTION

In almost every quest for publicity, one of the main objectives is to be granted a media interview — a showcase that will allow you to present your story to the public. It makes sense, therefore, to be well-prepared for handling an interview when the occasion actually arises. Understanding what is expected will help you make all the right moves.

This chapter will show you how to talk to the media, from the first telephone call you receive through a formal interview. In the next chapter, you'll expand your knowledge with some professional pointers on looking your best for television interviews.

b. BE PREPARED FOR THE TELEPHONE CALL

Once you start sending out publicity material, representatives of the media are likely to begin calling. There are four basic reasons they might telephone you:

Always be prepared for press reaction by having all necessary information close at hand.

(a) To verify information in your news release

(b) To get additional details about you or your organization

(c) To get a "quote" to go along with the story

(d) To arrange an in-depth interview.

Should you ever receive such a call, don't underestimate its importance. The way you handle the initial query can make all the difference in how your story is covered. Although they might appear to be casual requests, all journalistic inquiries should be taken very seriously.

Always be prepared for press reaction by having all necessary information at hand, or at least being able to get it quickly, just in case you do get a request for further details. Then make every effort to answer questions on the spot. Otherwise, you might lose your golden opportunity.

Even if you are occupied when you hear from the media, stop and give the caller your full attention if it is at all possible. After all, you're the one who initiated the contact by sending out a statement. If you appear to have lost interest, the media will, too.

c. THE PRE-INTERVIEW

Occasionally the first telephone call you receive in response to your publicity effort will actually be a thinly disguised audition or "pre-interview" interview, designed to see how well you would perform on the air or in an otherwise formal situation. In those cases, your remarks, including *what* you say as well as *how* you say it, will become the criteria for choosing you as an interview subject.

If the media does call regarding your publicity material, make the most of the occasion by treating the conversation as if it were a genuine broadcast performance.

◆ Be enthusiastic.

◆ Respond with short, lively answers.

◆ Speak up clearly.

◆ Avoid off-color expressions.

◆ Don't oversell your product by sounding like a commercial.

d. HAVE YOUR ANSWERS READY

If the caller requests an appointment for an interview or an appearance, you will probably want to think about your answers ahead of time. Since spontaneous statements are preferred by the majority of interviewers, however, most prefer not to divulge the nature of their questions in advance. You do have the right to know, before a long interview, the subjects in which the reporter is interested. And if the interviewer won't tell you, you can always try to second-guess what the questions might be.

Many journalists bristle, however, when told certain topics are "off limits," so don't try to control the topic.

Does agreeing to an interview obligate you to answer personal questions? It depends on whether the queries are actually relevant or merely rude. You certainly need not answer any questions that offend or embarrass you, but if you refuse to answer, try to appear polite and sincere rather than hostile.

e. NETIQUETTE

It's simply good manners to ask ahead of time if it's appropriate to give out your Web address during an interview. If so, you'll want to make sure the interviewer has the address ahead of time. On the other hand, it's quite possible the media wants to direct inquiries to its own site. If so, you'll want to ask for a link to your Web location, for people who want more information.

f. THE ABCs OF INTERVIEW SUCCESS

Being interviewed by the press should never be taken for granted; there is more to answering a journalist's questions than meets the eye. To present yourself in the best light during any interview, remember your ABCs: accuracy, brevity, and context.

1. Accuracy

Get your facts right, and use those facts to enhance your remarks. An opinion becomes an "expert opinion" when it's backed up by hard data. Know the important numbers — whether it's a quantity, date, time, or percentage. Accuracy doesn't require minute precision — you don't need the head count of a crowd, but if you say it was 12,000 when it was actually 1,200, reporters will soon cease to seek you out as a source.

2. Brevity

A short, simple answer is usually the best answer. That doesn't mean saying only "yes" or "no," however, because then you leave the reporter without any meaningful quotes. One or two sentences are adequate. If reporters want to hear more, they will ask a follow-up question.

3. Context

It's a frequent complaint: "I was quoted out of context." To help prevent that, listen to every question and make sure you understand it before you answer. There's nothing wrong with asking a reporter to clarify something you find ambiguous. It's better to let the reporter rephrase the question, than to guess what the reporter had in mind.

g. INTERVIEW TIPS

1. Be quotable

During an interview, one of your goals should be to say something quotable. Learning to speak in short sound bites will help journalists to pick out a good, memorable quote.

During an interview, one of your goals should be to say something significant that the media can later attribute to you in a quotation. Media experts do this by learning to turn their answers into quotable statements through one particular technique: incorporating the question into the answer. Read the following examples and then practice restating the question as part of your answer.

Question: Why did you decide to become a bridal consultant?

Weak answer: To help others.

Quotable answer: I decided to become a bridal consultant because, after planning the weddings for all 12 of my children, I wanted to put my experience to work for others.

Question: What advice do you have for others who might be thinking about opening their own bookstore?

Weak answer: Sign a short lease!

Quotable answer: For anyone thinking about opening a bookstore my advice would be, "Sign a short lease!"

2. Speak in sound bites

In taped or otherwise recorded interviews, the journalist's job is to reduce a great deal of information to a condensed version for print or broadcast purposes. Even though an interview can last for 45 minutes, the final story might be edited down to as few as 30 seconds on the air or 4 sentences in print.

Therefore, to become a sought-after media source, learn to keep your statements brief and to the point. As soon as you start to ramble, you make it difficult for a journalist to edit your response into usable form.

You can help your interviewer as well as yourself by always speaking in "sound bites" — 13- to 15-second remarks that make a point clearly and cogently. Even if it means practicing with a stopwatch, it pays to learn how to make every word count.

3.   Add color

You can liven up any discussion by using comparisons the audience can relate to. For example, rather than describing a product by its exact size and weight, make it more colorful by creating a picturesque image. Using such phrases as "It's the size of a compact car" or "It weighs about as much as a penny" gives the public something more to remember than straight statistics.

4.   Tips from the professionals

Career spokespersons and others whose job it is to speak to the press have learned the best ways to handle certain situations. From that experience, here are some guidelines designed to make media interviews less painful and more profitable.

For examples of how to answer questions, read the following suggestions and then, for additional examples, turn to Sample 18.

(a)   Talking "on the record"

The police are required to warn criminal suspects that anything they say can be used against them. Unfortunately, journalists don't offer any similar advice to interviewees. But if there were a media warning, it would be this: Always assume that everything you say is ON THE RECORD.

Regardless of the interview situation if *everything* you say is suitable for broadcast or publication, you will never have reason for embarrassment.

SAMPLE 18
ANSWERS TO DIFFICULT QUESTIONS

Although you might be interviewed several times without ever encountering a difficult or embarrassing question, it's a good idea to be prepared to answer such queries just in case the occasion should arise.

1. Personal questions

   Question: How much money did you earn last year?

   Incorrect response: That's none of your business.

   Correct response: That's a rather personal topic and I'd feel uncomfortable talking about it if you don't mind.

2. Negative comments

   Question: Why is your product better than your competition's?

   Incorrect response: My competition doesn't care about customer service.

   Correct answer: I can only speak for myself, and I try to maintain the highest standards in customer service.

3. Criticism

   Question: Why does the County Consumer Commission have 25 complaints against your company?

   Incorrect response: Oh, some people just like to complain.

   Correct response: We care about our customers and always try to see that they're satisfied. If people have complaints, I hope they'll bring them directly to us so that we can take care of them as quickly as possible.

4. Hypothetical questions

   Question: What if your license were taken away and you were forced to relocate to another state?

   Incorrect response: I would retire to the mountains and spend all my time fishing.

   Correct response: That's a hypothetical situation, and I'd rather wait to see what actually happens.

5. Telling the truth

   Question: How many widgets did you sell last year?

   Incorrect response: I don't remember.

   Correct response: I'm not sure of the answer to that, but I'll be glad to find out.

(b) Tell the truth

Whenever you are being interviewed by the media, always tell the truth. If you don't know the answer to a question, admit it. To maintain your credibility with members of the media, you must be truthful at all times.

(c) Avoid advertising

Keep in mind that an interview is not meant to be free advertising. Whether you're being questioned about a news story or are a guest on a television talk show, resist the temptation to push your product. Interviewers dislike "hard sell" tactics.

By avoiding bias toward specific brands and by allowing *the interviewer* to mention your product, you'll gain further credibility.

Always tell the truth when you are interviewed, or you will lose your credibility with the media.

(d) Think positively

It is unwise to speak negatively or critically of others during an interview because such statements tend to reflect unflatteringly on the speaker instead. Rather than portraying your competition as inferior, for example, emphasize your own strong points and leave your remarks at that.

(e) Hypothetical questions

Once your name appears in the news several times, the media will begin to perceive you as enough of an expert to call and ask for your opinion from time to time. Occasionally this means that you will be asked to discuss a difficult or sensitive subject. Although this is an opportunity for publicity, there can be pitfalls.

Whenever this happens, you can avoid a number of problems by following one simple rule: Never answer a hypothetical question.

h. PRACTICE, PRACTICE, PRACTICE

Very few people are "naturally" good at giving interviews. The experts are simply those individuals who have done it often enough to look natural. If you don't have the experience, though, you can gain the self-assurance you need by spending time practicing. Here's how to get the most out of your rehearsal.

1. Plan ahead

As an interview subject, you cannot control the date or time of your appearance in the media. But you do have dominion over two important factors: what you say and how you say it.

Each time you know in advance that you will be speaking with a writer or appearing on television, take time beforehand to plan certain remarks. That way, during the interview you will be able to make your points clearly and concisely. Then, regardless of when or where you are mentioned, your quotes will add sparkle to the story.

2. Brush up on your anecdotes

One way to score a hit with an audience is by relating colorful anecdotes during an interview. Even though you might not possess the skills of a professional raconteur, you can prepare for the task by asking yourself the following questions and then working the answers into your conversation.

(a) What are some of the most positive results you have had since you began offering your product or service?

(b) Which part of your job do you enjoy most?

(c) Describe the funniest thing that's happened to you in the course of running your business or organization.

(d) What is the most rewarding part of your job?

(e) Do you have any warnings for the public about (*fill in your type of business*)?

3. Try these rehearsal techniques

When you're alone, such as driving in your car, begin to spend time thinking up and answering some typical questions you're likely to face in an interview. Depending on what you're representing and who is questioning you, these will vary, but interviews usually include certain standard queries.

◆ Why did you start this company (organization, service)?

◆ What is unusual or unique about your product?

◆ Do you have any advice for consumers?

Answer yourself out loud. Listen to your answers, or better yet, tape record them. Rate your performance according to the following criteria:

- Do you speak in complete sentences?

- Are you providing interesting information or an opinion that you can back up with some data?

- Are you varying your vocal intonations?

- Do you manage to complete your thoughts within the 13- to 15-second "sound-bite" time frame?

- Do you sound comfortable rather than tense or nervous?

4. Review the dos and don'ts

Each time you are interviewed by the media, you will become more comfortable with the procedure and your responses will come more easily. But to ensure a polished performance every time, take a moment to review the reminders in Checklist 3.

i. ADD TO YOUR PUBLICITY PLANNER

To make the most of your rehearsal, write down the best answers that you come up with while practicing your "sound bite" techniques. Then try to work them into your responses so that they become automatic. Record them for reference by writing them down and storing them in a Publicity Planner file folder labelled "Interview notes." By preparing yourself this way before you are interviewed, you can easily review your notes even on very short notice.

CHECKLIST 3
INTERVIEW ETIQUETTE

Before you participate in any media interview, review the following helpful hints.

DO

- Have access to the data you need.
- Give the reporter your full attention.
- Assume that everything you say is "on the record."
- Tell the truth.
- Enhance your remarks with facts.
- Incorporate the question into the answer for more meaningful quotes.
- Answer questions within a 13- to 15-second time frame.

DON'T

- Make negative or critical remarks.
- Treat the interview as a free commercial.
- Answer hypothetical questions.
- Say anything "off the record."
- Stray from the subject.

11
POLISHING YOUR
TELEVISION IMAGE

a. INTRODUCTION

If you've been invited to appear on television, you've scored a home run in the publicity game. And regardless of whether it's an interview on the evening news, an appearance on local-access cable TV, or a guest spot on a nationally syndicated talk show, you'll want to look your best. That means learning inside secrets of television makeup and wardrobe techniques.

b. MAKEUP

1. Why makeup is needed

Applying makeup for television is not simply a matter of adding glamorous touches for a special occasion. It is a mandatory step for both men and women who are planning to go before the cameras. Everyone — from heads of state to former football players — wears makeup on TV because they want to appear healthy and vigorous, not pale, flat, and washed out. And so should you.

Television lights are very intense and will make you seem unhealthy and pale. Both men and women need to wear makeup for television interviews.

Makeup is necessary because television lights are very intense. The brightness of the lights improves the quality of the picture but, at the same time, overpowers the natural color of the skin, often casting a faint blue tint that is anything but healthy-looking. Even in "natural" or low-light situations, the camera itself washes out some of the intensity, meaning you have to compensate by adding color to your skin.

2. Do-it-yourself makeup

For most of your appearances on television, you will have to do your own makeup. In television news, as well as in most other local programming, makeup artists are rare. So be sure to ask before your appearance whether or not someone will be available to apply your makeup, because unless you're specifically told otherwise, you will be entirely responsible for your own appearance.

In addition, since you probably won't have a chance to do more than add powder after you get to the television studio, plan to look your best *before* you arrive.

3. Makeup basics

Before you face the cameras, here are some quick guidelines for both men and women on makeup application:

(a) Start with a good concealer, preferably one with a yellow tint, to neutralize the red or purple color of dark circles and blemishes. Apply it under the eyes and to any noticeable discolorations.

(b) Even if you wear makeup every day, do not use your normal color for television. Choose a shade with a slightly orange tint to compensate for the blue cast of the television lights. This is true for all skin tones.

(c) Apply makeup with a cosmetic sponge, making sure to carry the color over to include exposed areas of your throat, hairline, and even ear lobes. Makeup should not end abruptly, as the difference in tone will show.

(d) To bring out cheekbones, a touch of iridescent or very light-colored highlighter can be applied just under the outer edge of the eye, atop the peak of the cheekbone.

(e) For most appearances, men need only follow those steps with a light coating of translucent face powder patted on to prevent shine. For those men with receding hairlines, the top of the head also requires both foundation and powder.

4. Makeup tips for women only

When appearing on television, many women prefer to brighten their natural color slightly more than men do by adding cheek blush, eye makeup, and lipstick. The following guidelines have been designed to help achieve the best effects. For a complete checklist of colors, see Checklist 4.

(a) Blusher and lipstick

Use cheek blusher and lipstick that complement the colors of your clothing. A maroon blouse, for example, will start a color war with an apricot blush because one is cool while the other is warm. If you're wearing clothing with a blue or rose undertone, therefore, choose a blusher in the same family. If your clothing falls in the warm category, with gold or yellow undertones, select warm colors for your makeup.

(b) Eye shadow

Avoid blue, purple, green and other unnatural skin colors for eyelids. Instead, choose colors like charcoal, taupe, gray, and brown to create more natural contours and shadows. If you want to add a highlight color just below the eyebrow, opt for subtle, skin-tone shades like pale peach or light rose for light- and medium-toned skin; copper or rust for bronze and dark skin tones.

(c) Color blending

Make your colors slightly more intense for television than you would for the office by applying more makeup than usual. But before you finish, be sure to blend the edges of your blush, eyeliner, and eye shadow very carefully. There should be no sharp lines between colors.

(d) Lipstick

Using a lip pencil one shade darker than your lipstick is a good idea because it defines the shape of your mouth and helps to contain the color. When choosing lipstick, avoid very dark shades, especially

CHECKLIST 4
TELEVISION APPEARANCE CHECKLIST

	PREFERRED	AVOID
Concealer	Yellow-tinted	White
Foundation	Orange-tinted	Tints that match natural skin tone
	Highlighter to add dimension	Pale shades
Blush	Soft colors: rose, peach with darker shades for contour	Burgundy and other deep, blue-based reds
Eyeliner and mascara	Black, charcoal, brown	Blue
Eye shadow	Shadow: darker shades of rust, brown, taupe, gray	Medium or light blues and bright, spring green
	Highlighter: soft shades of off-white, peach, light pink, soft gold, copper	Bright colors
Lip colors	Muted shades: plum, watermelon, rose, ruby, garnet	Burgundy, violet, pale pastels, gloss
Clothing, patterns	Solid colors, soft patterns	Sharp or small patterns, tight stripes, geometric design, chevron tweeds
Clothing, colors	Intense shades: burgundy, teal, blue, rich yellow, rust, reds, purple	White; colors that blend into natural skin tones
Jewelry	Brushed or satin finish; pearls; non-reflective metals	Flat, shiny surfaces; dangling earrings; large pendants; noisy beads, bracelets
Eyeglasses	Glare-resistant lenses; plastic frames	Dark-tinted lenses; metal frames

those with a purple or blue undertone. Remember that the lights are somewhat blue already, and the effect can be ghoulish if you're not careful. Also, stay away from glossy lipstick and never add lip gloss; the shine can be very distracting on television.

(e) Powder

Always finish your makeup routine with a light dusting of translucent powder. If you apply your makeup more than 20 minutes before the interview, re-apply the powder before you face the cameras.

c. CLOTHING

After you have been called on to appear on television, one of the most important decisions you will make is choosing what to wear. You know that in everyday life some clothing colors are more flattering than others, but for television you need to consider several other factors as well.

1. Color

In general, solid colors work best on television. Stripes, tight patterns, and geometric designs all tend to cause visual "vibrations" on the screen, a distracting zig-zag pattern called a "moire effect."

2. Avoid white

The only exception to the solid color rule is white; never wear solid white on television. It "flares," causing a shutdown of the camera iris which, in turn, will make you look dark and shadowy. A small amount of white, as in a collar, piping or a pocket handkerchief, is acceptable. But if you're wearing a white shirt or blouse when the TV crew shows up, change it if possible. Or, at the very least, put on a jacket.

3. Style

When choosing your on-camera clothing, be yourself, within limits. Wear the colors and styles that are right for you, not necessarily the ones your own favorite TV personality wears. Your personal best should be based on your own individual coloring and must complement you. Therefore mimicking someone else's taste in wardrobe will never be successful.

Make sure to choose your television wardrobe carefully. Certain colors and patterns cause visual distractions and should be avoided.

The same is also true for the *style* of clothing you choose, whether that means a high neckline, a round collar, or — for men — a bow tie. Just remember that your style should never be so extreme that it will create a distraction for viewers.

4. Appropriate attire

Dressing appropriately for television means wearing correct clothing for your type of business. A store owner would look out of place in formal evening dress while working behind the counter. And a civic leader would appear much too casual being interviewed while wearing a T-shirt and shorts.

5. For men only

When choosing attire for television, men should make a point to wear knee-high stockings. That way, if they are seated and their trousers should rise above their shoes, their legs will be covered.

d. ACCESSORIES

When you're in front of cameras, whether for still photographs or television, your goal should be to look your best *without creating a distraction:* no dark sunglasses, no overpowering jewelry, no unusual hats. To create the best impression, the secret is to keep your accessories conservative.

1. Jewelry

Choose a "stealth" design — that is, one without large, reflecting, shiny surfaces. Brushed metal is less likely to catch the lights and cause an unwanted reflection.

Make sure your jewelry isn't noisy. Two or three strands of beads can create an annoying, clicking sound whenever you move that will be magnified by the microphones.

Avoid jewelry that "moves." Dangling earrings and swinging pendants have a tendency to draw the audience's attention away from what you're saying.

2. Hats

Don't wear a hat on television if you can help it. Hats can cast shadows across your face and make it impossible for the camera operator to focus on your features.

3. Eyeglasses

Manufacturers now offer eyeglass lenses that are glare resistant and very suitable for television. If you plan to appear on camera, consider having your regular lenses replaced. If you do not have specially treated lenses, try to work with the camera operator to reduce glare by tilting your glasses downward, if necessary. Also, avoid metal frames when possible; they're more likely to cause a reflection.

e. BODY LANGUAGE

Although many television interviews are known as "talking heads," which means the camera only shows the participants from the shoulders up, the way you sit or stand can still make a difference in how you look. For example, the positioning of your body can determine whether you appear to have a full face, a short neck, or broad shoulders.

Before you appear on television, try to find a comfortable position that allows you to keep your back straight, your shoulders relaxed, and your head up. Practice ahead of time by sitting or standing in front of a full-length mirror. Strive for an attentive look and erect posture. Then close your eyes and try to remember how it feels to be in the proper position.

f. FULL DRESS REHEARSAL

If you are planning a major publicity tour to promote your project, it would benefit you to rehearse as fully as possible ahead of time. In order to accomplish this, you will need to enlist the aid of at least two other people.

First, find someone to play the role of your interviewer and to ask you questions you have designed for the purpose. Second, if possible, have a friend videotape your rehearsal so that you can see how you will actually appear. If no camera is available, try to practice in front of a mirror.

During the rehearsal, pay particular attention to three aspects of your on-screen behavior:

◆ Remember to look at the interviewer, *not* the camera.

◆ Find a natural, resting position for your hands.

◆ Never fidget or exhibit any nervous mannerisms.

g. WHAT TO EXPECT AT A TV STUDIO

If you are invited to appear at a television studio for your interview, knowing what to expect ahead of time can help to calm any fears. Most stations ask guests to wait, at least for a few minutes, in what is called the "green room." Don't be surprised if it's not green, or even if it's not a room. "Green room" is just the television term for the waiting area.

When it's time for your interview, you will be escorted into a studio where the crew will offer you a seat and a microphone. Occasionally a technician will ask you to adjust your clothing or remove your jacket for a moment in order to hide the microphone cable.

If your appearance is part of a program being produced elsewhere — that is, if you're only facing a camera rather than an interviewer — you'll be given an ear piece called an IFB. Work with the crew to make sure it's comfortable and securely in place and that the volume is loud enough for you to hear. Following that, the interviewer or producer will usually speak with you for a few minutes about the program's focus. And finally, it's lights, camera, action!

During the interview, the studio crew will use gestures to signal the interviewer which camera to turn to and how much time is left. Just ignore their signs and focus on your conversation. Everything else will take care of itself.

h. LAST-MINUTE APPEARANCES

Many times, especially with TV news, interviews are conducted "in the field." This simply means that a crew will record the interview somewhere other than a television studio. So don't be surprised, once you become a familiar face to the media, if you get a call asking if a reporter can drop by in an hour or two to conduct an interview for immediate airing.

In fact, if you have one or two appropriate outfits for television, it would be wise to keep them at hand. And once it seems a possibility that you and the media will definitely be seeing more of each other, you should also be ready to apply your TV makeup on short notice. Cooperating with the media can be your key to success.

To prepare yourself for an interview, try rehearsing with a few friends. Make a list of questions that you may be asked, and practice answering them.

i. ADD TO YOUR PUBLICITY PLANNER

If you should receive a call requesting a television interview, you will want to be prepared. So go through your wardrobe and makeup now to see if you need to add anything.

First, on a piece of paper, list the clothing and accessories you own that would be most suitable for a television interview. Include the jacket, the shirt, the jewelry, the belt, the shoes, and other items that complete the outfit. If necessary, consider purchasing the requisite wardrobe.

Next, practice putting on TV makeup a few times and write down the colors you are using. If you don't have any translucent powder, make sure you buy some and keep it on hand.

Finally, store this wardrobe and makeup information in the "Interview notes" file of your Publicity Planner. When that all-important phone call comes in asking for a television interview, you'll be able to pull out one file and have all your necessary information at hand.

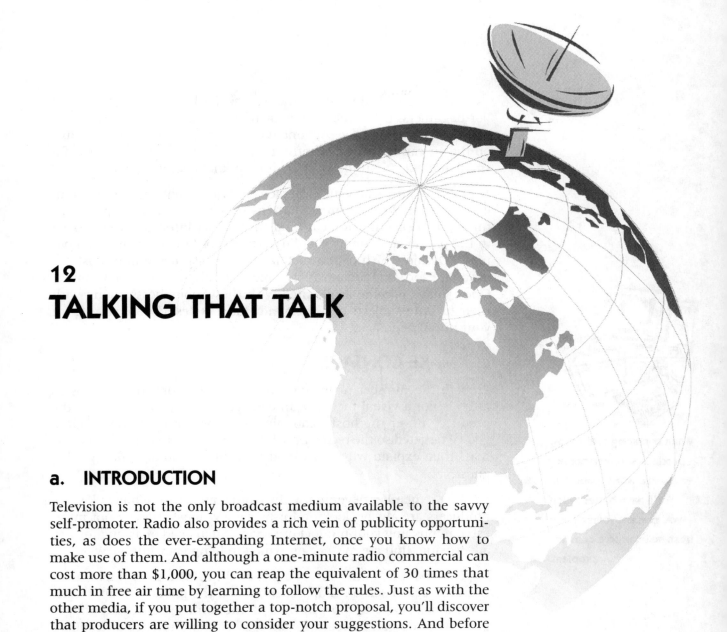

12
TALKING THAT TALK

a. INTRODUCTION

Television is not the only broadcast medium available to the savvy self-promoter. Radio also provides a rich vein of publicity opportunities, as does the ever-expanding Internet, once you know how to make use of them. And although a one-minute radio commercial can cost more than $1,000, you can reap the equivalent of 30 times that much in free air time by learning to follow the rules. Just as with the other media, if you put together a top-notch proposal, you'll discover that producers are willing to consider your suggestions. And before long, you'll become a regular on the radio and Internet chat show circuit.

b. BEGIN AT THE BEGINNING

To be a guest on radio, whether local, regional, or nationally broadcast, you don't have to be a famous author, a well-known movie star, or an influential politician. Regardless of your specialty, you can find a program with your name on it by simply researching the radio market.

Where should you start your quest for this broadcasting bonanza? For beginners, try to rehearse your routine on the local level before taking it to the big time. Anyone who has ever been interviewed live on the air can tell you: It's better to learn the ropes first in front of a small audience than to get all tied up in knots before millions.

First, write or call your local radio stations to obtain their program guides. (Even 24-hour music stations sometimes offer talk programming on weekends.) You can find the contact information you need in the phone book under "Radio Stations" or "Broadcasting Companies." Decide which of the vast array of talk shows sound most appropriate for your organization's message, then listen a few times. Once you've become acquainted with the various hosts, along with their favorite subjects and their individual styles, choose several for your initial approach.

c. MAKE CONTACT

Prepare the number of media kits you'll need, omitting photos as radio is not a visual medium. In each cover letter (addressed to the producer, never the host), compliment some aspect of the program you've targeted so the recipient will know you're familiar with the format. Then explain why you would be a timely and attention-getting guest.

Just remember never to use the word "publicity." While talk show producers are always looking for lively new ideas, they're not interested in pushing your product or service. So instead of asking for free advertising, find a news peg on which to hang your interview.

For example, in the spring a personal fitness trainer might mention that beach season is approaching and the public will appreciate some quick shape-up tips. In the fall, the same expert could offer to give advice on getting ready for ski season. Nonprofit groups can also provide valuable, up-to-date advice to listeners, from the latest medical news to the hottest trends in home offices. In either case, by presenting yourself as a fresh solution to a common problem, you'll have a better chance of being chosen.

d. WRITE YOUR OWN SCRIPT

More than another other medium, radio requires lively and colorful conversation to prevent listeners from tuning out. So once you're booked, plan to practice (using a stop watch and a tape recorder) to

When contacing radio show producers, remember not to use the word "publicity." You'll have better luck if you present yourself as a fresh solution to a common problem.

get into the rhythm of answering questions in concise 15- to 30-second sound bites. Guests who are ill-prepared or who ramble on endlessly before coming to the point are never invited back.

To insure success, memorize a number of humorous or helpful anecdotes ahead of time. Then, should the program wander far afield or even take an unpleasant turn, you can always insert your prepared comments into the conversation. If a caller should ask an embarrassing question, you could respond by saying, "I don't know the answer to that, but let me tell you the funniest (or most important or most dangerous or most valuable) advice I've ever heard on that subject."

By having a script in your head, you can more easily lead the interview in the direction you choose. This technique worked exceptionally well for a woman entrepreneur who was annoyed by a talk show host who kept asking inappropriate questions. When he finally paused for breath she immediately interjected, "You know, one question I'm asked a lot is ..." From that point on, she was in control and able to steer the conversation where she wanted it to go.

e. AVOID ADVERTISING

As with all media interviews, never treat a radio spot like a commercial. Your host wants only to entertain the audience, not to sell your merchandise. Your job is to be charming, clever, and colorful. If you're a likable guest, listeners will respond positively to your product or service. But allow the host to promote you and your organization graciously with the comments written on his cue cards.

If you do have details which the host isn't aware of, such as a special phone number listeners can call, ask if you can give it out over the air. Make it easy on the audience, though, by allowing them time to find a pencil. Then state the information slowly and clearly — twice.

f. WORLD WITHOUT WALLS

Amazingly, most of the one million radio interviews conducted annually don't even take place in a studio. Thanks to modern technology, the vast majority are conducted by telephone from wherever the guest happens to be at the time — at home thousands of miles from the station, driving down the street in a car, or even in the bathtub. (It's true. One veteran of the airwaves takes pride in dispensing advice while up to his eyeballs in soap bubbles.)

Due the existence of long-distance radio appearances, it is now possible to be "live" on the air in Montreal while lounging poolside in Miami.

Because it's now possible to be "live" on the air in snowy Montreal at the same time you're poolside in steamy Miami, making a name for yourself on the radio is easier than ever. To find out which talk shows await you, check the media guides in your local library (and on the Internet). You'll find the names, addresses, producers, and telephone numbers for more than a thousand programs, all of which need an endless supply of guests.

When arranging a remote interview, which is the industry term for long-distance radio appearances, you'll need to schedule a date and time with the program's producer. Since these programs can cross a number of time zones, make it quite clear what time it will be for both of you. If you're not familiar with the show because it's not broadcast in your area, be sure to ask about the format, the audience, the length of the interview, any other guests, and the types of questions the host will ask.

Find out if it's a call-in show so you'll be ready to respond. And most important, always ask for a telephone number in the studio which you can call in case you get disconnected during the broadcast. Despite everyone's best intentions, accidents do happen and you need to be ready to take action.

On the day of the actual remote interview, you'll receive a phone call a few minutes ahead of time and, after a brief wait, you'll hear the radio personality introduce you. At the same time you're carrying on your conversation with the host, your voice will be broadcast. When callers are invited to participate, you'll hear them through the phone. Remember to relate your responses to the time of day where the audience is located.

To sound your best, be seated comfortably in a quiet room with no ringing bells, chiming clocks, crying babies, or barking dogs. Always turn off your call-waiting feature so no extraneous sounds will interfere. Finally, make sure you have all your necessary reference materials close at hand, including pen and paper for keeping track of important facts, such as the host's name.

g. IN THE STUDIO

If your interview will take place at a radio station, don't be intimidated by the equipment in the studio. Someone will demonstrate how to speak into the microphone and you'll be given headphones to hear caller questions. Be prepared to give your business card to the switchboard operator as you leave the radio station and politely ask to have any inquiries referred to you. Many talk shows don't have a designated individual to handle follow-up calls, which means important connections might fall through the cracks.

h. RULES TO REMEMBER

When being interviewed on the air, always assume your microphone or telephone line is open and broadcasting. Never, never say anything aloud — to the host, to yourself, or to someone in your house — assuming that you're speaking in private. By the same token, refrain from commenting on the commercials in any way. Focus completely on getting your message out and save your personal asides until the program has ended.

Also, occasionally when the audience is invited to participate, a prank caller will say something offensive or even obscene. Should this ever happen while you're a guest, just keep quiet and let the host handle the situation. They're trained to deal with such annoyances.

Following every interview, once you're back home or at the office, immediately send a thank you note to the producer and another to the host. Don't mention the "free publicity" aspect, but let them know you enjoyed the experience. Enclose a business or Rolodex card and be sure to say you'd love to be invited back again.

The rules of Internet chatrooms are constantly changing, so make sure you are clear on all the details before you become a chatroom guest.

i. THE CHATROOM EXPERIENCE

The rules of Internet chatrooms are constantly changing. You can't take anything for granted. For example, some Internet chatroom hosts will provide a typist for you, so that you conduct something more like a telephone interview. The typist is on the other end of a phone line, rapidly putting your words on the screen. Other sites expect you to do your own typing. Chatroom participants might be quite limited, or the discussion could by open to anyone on the Web. Some sites will screen the comments and queries before they're displayed, others will allow the conversation to go wherever the participants want. As with all media appearances, you'll want to maintain a professional demeanor, and allow the host to exercise control over the chat's direction.

When you're invited to be a chatroom guest find out as much as you can about the format ahead of time. Who are the other participants? How long will the chat run? What's the focus and the tone of the chatroom? Is this going to be an actual, live exchange, or is it merely a place where questions and answers will be shown? Is the chat going to be archived? That way, you can make the most of the opportunity by being prepared. Just as you would for any other interview, you need to practice giving short, high-impact responses. This is is no time for long explanations, just highlights. Make sure you save the chatroom experience for your own records, because it can help you polish your style and improve your performance.

j. ADD TO YOUR PUBLICITY PLANNER

Keep track, in chronological order, of all your guest spots. For TV and radio, it's important to keep track of the station name, address, program name, producer, date, time, host, fax and telephone numbers and any comments you want to make. After Internet appearances, print out the chatroom exchange that featured you and make sure you have all relevant Web addresses on file. Put it in your "Media List" folder and refer to it whenever you have news you think any of them might want to know.

13
PUBLIC SPEAKING FOR PUBLICITY AND PROFIT

a. INTRODUCTION

When you are seeking ways to make your name better known to the public — whether in your local community or on a national basis — one of the best solutions you will find is public speaking. Not only does speaking before groups afford an excellent opportunity for publicity, but it can also generate extra income.

This chapter will demonstrate the value of public speaking, both as a promotional tool and as a method of increasing your profits. You will learn several ways to make public speaking a regular part of your publicity program, how to prepare your presentations, and where to find your potential audiences.

Regardless of your education or occupation, you can profit from public-speaking opportunities. In fact, with practice, you might even be able to turn lecturing into a lucrative sideline that increases your income and your public profile at the same time.

Public speaking allows you to introduce yourself and your endeavor to the public, and to spread the word much quicker than one-to-one communication.

b. THE BENEFITS OF PUBLIC SPEAKING

Public speaking, whether formal or informal, has a number of advantages for both business and nonprofit concerns. First, it provides a showcase for you to introduce yourself and your endeavor to the public. Second, by allowing you to talk to many people at once, it helps spread the word faster than one-to-one communication. And, finally, it gives you an opportunity to publicize yourself in the media by supplying you with a promotable activity.

Although you might think of public speaking strictly in terms of delivering a serious lecture to a large audience, in actual practice it also includes a number of less formal occasions as well. Here are some of the most frequent opportunities for public speaking:

(a) Presenting a short talk to social clubs, business organizations, and fraternal groups interested in your topic

(b) Giving an after-dinner speech at the monthly meeting of some type of professional organization

(c) Being chosen for a panel discussion organized to present information to a particular group of individuals

(d) Conducting a workshop

(e) Participating in a high school's "career day" events where students learn about different occupations

(f) Speaking at a seminar held during a convention or trade show

(g) Teaching a class

(h) Delivering a formal speech in a large auditorium

If you're wondering how any of these activities might actually help to build your business, add to your income, or increase public awareness of your organization, examples abound. For instance, a landscape designer who conducts classes on backyard gardening says he regularly acquires new customers not only from among his students, but from their friends as well. Likewise, a management consultant reports that she gains new clients every time she participates in entrepreneurship seminars sponsored by her local government.

A construction contractor has discovered that it pays him to teach a home building course because he not only earns a salary, he attracts new clients to his firm at the same time. And one home-based business owner actually increased her income from $5 an hour as a typist to $100,000 a year by conducting workshops on how to start an in-home business.

c. BEGIN WITH THE BASICS

If you've never lectured or taught before, you'll probably find it most comfortable to begin by addressing small groups, choosing informal occasions, or participating in a panel discussion rather than speaking alone. Then as you become more comfortable with the situation, you might want to move up to larger audiences, more formal settings, or even to full-time paid public speaking, as more than one entrepreneurial-minded individual has done.

In any case, the first step is to become acquainted with the opportunities that exist in your immediate area. If a classroom situation appeals to you, begin by calling your local educational institutions and inquiring about non-credit teaching positions in your field of expertise.

If club meetings seem more suited to your talents, then ask at the chamber of commerce or other community associations for information about groups that might be interested in having speakers.

Contact appropriate government agencies to see if they ever sponsor educational, business, career, or professional seminars in which you could participate as a speaker or workshop leader.

If it's appropriate, check with the recreation department where you live to find out if there are any outdoor programs that use guest lecturers.

Whenever you find an opportunity that sounds suitable, offer your services over the telephone. If the person you're talking to says the group needs a more formal proposal, send them a media kit (without a press release). They'll undoubtedly be impressed with your presentation.

Finally, consider putting on a lecture right in your own store or office. Whether it's a fifteen-minute demonstration of computer equipment or a one-hour discussion on estate planning, you'll find it valuable because it actually brings people into your place of business.

d. DESIGN A PRESENTATION

Once you decide to try your hand at public speaking, your first challenge will be to develop your presentation. Several simple tips will help you organize your speech and get you started in the right direction.

1. Answer consumer questions

Whether you are designing a five-minute talk or an eight-week course, plan your remarks to answer consumer questions about your subject, not to sell your own products and services. As a business owner, you are familiar with the most common questions your customers ask. A good speech will simply answer those questions.

If you own an accounting firm, for example, you should not try to sell your services to the people in the audience, but instead you should address their *consumer* questions, such as how many years they must keep their canceled checks. Or, if you own a clothing boutique, rather than recommending certain brands, you might offer guidelines for "finding your own style." In one suburb, a paint store holds occasional evening seminars on professional house painting techniques while a medical clinic offers free lectures on good eye care.

Remember that a speech is not a sales talk. A speech is simply an opportunity for you to educate consumers and attempt to generate a little good will.

2. Emphasize only a few main points

Before you write your speech, sit down and think about the five or ten things you would tell all of your customers if you had the opportunity. Would you advise them to clean their furnace filters more often? Would you suggest that they buy their running shoes one size larger than their dress shoes? Would you tell them what to look for when buying a camera?

List those hints on a piece of paper and you have the basis for your presentation. In a very short talk, you might even address only one topic, such as "The Best Way to ...." By emphasizing only a few main points, your lecture will be cohesive and make a strong impression on the audience.

Remember: a speech is not a sales talk. Educate consumers and generate a little good will, but don't push your product.

3. Use visuals

You can make almost any presentation livelier by including some type of "prop" or visual aid. It can be one of your products, a poster-sized photograph, an informative chart, or any other visually exciting object. Just make sure that whatever you choose is large enough for everyone to see and that it enhances your presentation in some way. But avoid exhibits that require you to turn out the lights or set up a projector, as they tend to slow the pace.

e. GET THE WORDS RIGHT

Unless you have been selected to deliver a keynote address, treat your presentation as a one-on-one conversation. Take your list of main points with you and try to mention them all. But rather than reading from a written page or memorizing a long speech, talk to your audience as if they were customers shopping in your store or asking for your advice. Your natural enthusiasm for your subject will earn the audience's respect and help prevent you from becoming nervous.

Of course, to make the best impression, you should rehearse your presentation ahead of time. Always allow time to practice aloud before the actual performance. By doing so, you'll not only become more comfortable with the content, you'll know how long your speech lasts in case members of the group want to know.

Also, always plan to ask for questions from the audience at the end of your talk. If you're friendly and approachable, you'll not only gain new customers, you'll lay the groundwork for future speaking offers as well.

But if you think you could use a little help before venturing out on the lecture circuit, just attend a few club meetings, classes, or seminars yourself and pay attention to the interaction. It will give you a clear idea of what an audience expects as well as what type of presentation to prepare.

f. GIVEAWAYS

Each and every time you appear as a speaker, take two items with you. First, always have a press kit in case a member of the media is in attendance. Second, take along some sort of souvenir to give to audience members at the end of your presentation.

Whether you hand out your business card, your brochure, a packet of information specially prepared for the occasion, or even a pen carrying your company emblem, always be prepared with enough items for everyone in the audience and a few extras to take to their friends. That way your presentation will create a more lasting impression, and it will be easier for interested individuals to contact you.

g. TURN PUBLIC SPEAKING INTO PUBLICITY

If, by now, you've decided that you want to make the most of public speaking, then you'll also want to get as much publicity as possible out of every undertaking. That means sending press releases from time to time regarding your speaking engagements. And, it means listing your upcoming appearances on your Web site.

Each time you speak at a seminar, teach a course, conduct a workshop, or deliver a presentation to a group, you actually have your choice of two opportunities to send news releases — one before the event announcing that it will take place and another after it's over describing the outcome. But if you plan to speak often, you won't want to send too many releases or you'll blunt their effect. Instead, send one news release only regarding each speech. Once you've notified one particular media outlet, don't send any more speech-related releases to that target.

Once people begin to see your name mentioned in *various* places as a speaker, you might even begin to get invitations to appear before more groups.

h. ADD TO YOUR PUBLICITY PLANNER

If teaching a course or speaking to groups appeals to you as a promotional activity, then you need to label a new folder in your Publicity Planner to hold the appropriate materials. Call it "Public speaking/Teaching" and use it to file your lecture notes as well as a sample of the promotional items you plan to give away at each appearance.

In addition, keep a list of all the places you speak, the dates of the appearances, and the topics. And once you have delivered a number of talks, if you find that you are able to give the same presentation to most groups with only a few changes, you might want to write and store permanent outlines for lectures of different lengths. That way, preparing for each speech will require a minimum of time.

14
WRITING AS A PUBLICITY TOOL

a. INTRODUCTION

Like teaching classes or giving speeches, writing for publication can also provide a unique vehicle for publicity purposes, not only by getting your name into the media, but also by helping you to earn extra money and enhancing your professional reputation. Although you might believe that you lack the necessary qualifications to become a published writer, don't feel intimidated. There are many ways of breaking into print and you might be surprised to find how many you can use.

In this chapter you will learn how to give your writing a professional look, where to get it published, and how to use your byline to boost your business.

b. WIN PUBLICITY WITH YOUR PEN

Can writing something for publication actually bring publicity to you or your organization? The answer is yes.

Everyone who needs the public to survive can increase visibility and enhance his or her image by having something published.

First, when you have something published, your name as author is usually printed right at the top of the page, which means that nearly everyone who reads the publication will see it. In addition, many magazines, newspapers, trade journals, and newsletters also print a brief "biographical note," adding even further to your name recognition.

Second, every time you have something published you create the opportunity to send a press release announcing your achievement.

Third, being published increases the public perception of you as someone of note, an expert in your field. You gain credibility when a publication seemingly "endorses" your viewpoint by allowing you space in its pages.

But who can benefit from this type of activity? Everyone who needs the public to survive can increase visibility and enhance his or her image by having something published.

As an example, an artist wrote an article about a sketching technique she developed, which was published in a magazine for professional painters. Then she sent a press release *about* the article to her hometown newspaper and to her college alumni magazine. Both publications mentioned not only her article, but her artwork as well, resulting in actual sales for the artist.

In another situation, a real estate agent's commentary on sales techniques appeared in a real estate trade magazine. He sent that article, along with a cover letter and a press release, to a community newspaper, which sent a reporter and published a feature article on him.

The variations are endless. But the results are the same: writing for publication is a cost-effective promotional tool that also provides multiple opportunities for publicity.

c. VARIOUS FORMS OF WRITING

Don't be intimidated because you think you need to produce a long, complex composition to have something worth publishing. In fact, writing for publication can take a wide variety of forms, from a two-sentence household hint to a full-fledged book. Even a letter can be used to generate publicity. As you assess your own writing abilities, consider putting some of the following ideas down on paper.

1.   A letter to the editor

Whether you want to state an opinion, elicit support for a project, or thank members of your community for their help, writing a letter to the editor, signed with your name and title as well as the name of your organization, can bring instant attention. In fact, newspapers and magazines occasionally telephone letter writers to interview them for articles.

2.   A hint, tip, or suggestion

Watch for columns in magazines and newspapers that print suggestions from readers along with the readers' names and locations. If you think of a clever or original idea, send it along. Even that kind of media mention can bring a surprising amount of attention to you, and then become the basis for sending a press release.

3.   A numbered list of consumer tips

Start with a title like "Ten Ways to ..." or "Five Methods of ..." dealing specifically with your specialty, then just write a paragraph (or even a sentence) on each. A travel agency owner might write about little-known tourist bargains or a financial consultant might offer advice on saving money for a college education. Base the tips on the questions your customers ask you most often and you will have an instant article suitable for any number of publications.

4.   A regular column

Have you ever wanted to write your own column in a newspaper or magazine? If so, sit down and write three or four and mail them to an editor along with a letter explaining that you are interested in becoming a regular columnist. If you prefer the question-and-answer format, make up questions just like those your customers ask you.

One woman who owns a garden supply shop writes a weekly article in a suburban newspaper about the latest trends in backyard gardening. Similarly, a lawyer provides written answers to questions for the real estate section of a community newspaper. Look through your own newspapers and you'll probably find several spots where you can contribute too.

5.   An article

If you really enjoy writing, you might want to put together a regular article, just like those you see every day in print. Depending on where you hope to see it published, you can write an essay, an interview, a travel feature, a how-to article or even a first-person narrative based on some exciting incident in your life. It doesn't necessarily have to be related to your business, but be sure to include the name of your company in the biography you send, as explained in section **d. Rules for Writing.**

6. A book

Some business owners have actually written books, had them published, gained publicity, and attracted new customers to their firms. One landscaper has even parlayed his publishing success into a second career by putting out a series of books, all based on his knowledge of plants and trees.

Submitting a book proposal to a publisher is not that different from submitting an article, except that you need to include a detailed outline of the entire book and, sometimes, at least two completed chapters. Publishers often will send you guidelines for submissions on request.

d. RULES FOR WRITING

If you would like to try your hand at producing something for publication, there are a few rules to which you will have to adhere to have your manuscript read.

(a) Begin with a one-page cover letter typed on your business stationery, introducing yourself.

(b) Everything must be typed. The cover letter may be single spaced but the article must be double spaced. Both need margins of at least one inch all the way around.

(c) Use only good quality white paper and black ink for the article.

(d) For submissions of more than two pages, do not fold, but send them flat in large envelopes.

(e) Everything you submit must be *completely* original.

(f) Number the article pages at the top and type your name and address, single spaced, in the top left-hand corner of every page.

(g) Include a biography similar to the one in your press kit.

(h) Enclose copies of any previous writing you have had published.

(i) If you are submitting a one- or two-page article, simply send it to the section editor of a newspaper or magazine. But if you are proposing a longer article or a book, it is more acceptable to send a query letter rather than a finished article. A query letter is a cover letter describing your article and your credentials for writing it. In it you should say whom you plan to interview; where you did research; the number of words of the finished article; and why readers of that particular publication would be interested.

(j) Always enclose a self-addressed, stamped envelope large enough for the editor to return the entire submission.

e. MARKETS

Just as with your other publicity efforts, you will need to build your reputation as a writer from small, local publications to larger outlets with national circulations. Before your submissions will be welcomed at the most prestigious publications — national magazines and large metropolitan daily newspapers — you will need to prove yourself by having your writing printed in publications with smaller readership.

Don't be afraid to start at the bottom rung and work your way up the ladder of literary success; every time your name appears in print you are a winner. Even if you begin with a short piece in your club newsletter for which you receive no payment, you will still increase your visibility in three ways: as a writer, as an expert in your field, and as a leader in your organization.

f. ADD TO YOUR PUBLICITY PLANNER

If you should decide to try your hand at writing for publication, prepare for it ahead of time by labelling a folder in your Publicity Planner "Writing opportunities." In it you can file ideas of your own when you think of them and also save articles written by others as inspiration for columns of your own. Then, one day when things are quiet, you'll be able to sit down and start work on your very first piece of published writing.

As you mail your submissions and query letters, always keep a copy in this file. And when you succeed in getting into print, create one more file folder labelled "Published writing."

15
POLISHING YOUR PUBLICITY TECHNIQUES

a. INTRODUCTION

As you look forward to your contacts with the media, you'll want to be aware of every technique that can work to your advantage, from the specifics of how to talk to the media to the rules about scheduling a media event to maximize coverage.

In this chapter you will learn some of the advanced techniques that will enhance your publicity drives and help you attract more and more attention. You might never need some of this information, but it's important that you understand the techniques in case you do.

b. ESTABLISH CORDIAL MEDIA RELATIONS

A good relationship with the press doesn't require you to invite reporters to lunch once a week or take them to the golf course on weekends. Rather, a good relationship is one in which the reporter recognizes *and respects* your efforts, both in your business and in your

To maintain good media contacts, focus on your personal standards of reliability and integrity, rather than on becoming "chummy" with people in the media. And remember — you're always "on the record."

media contacts. Achieving this is related more to how well you uphold standards of reliability and integrity than how "chummy" you are with individuals in the media.

It is advisable to be friendly and cordial to members of the media, of course, but within the confines of any business relationship. Keep in mind that, in this case, even when the reporter invites casual banter, you're speaking "on the record," not privately to an individual.

1.   It's not your show

When you send out a stack of press releases, you'll have an idea of how you'd like to see the item treated by the media. But once those mailings leave your hands, so does control over the subject. If an editor, reporter, or producer takes an interest in your suggestion, it's entirely up to that individual — and those who work with him or her — to decide how the subject will be handled. The worst thing you can do is make an effort to control what is said, how it's said, where the coverage is placed, how much time or space is given, and who else is contacted in the process. Simply put, it's not your show. You control what *you* say, and that's all you can do.

2.   When all is said and done

Because most news reporters cherish the image of themselves as objective observers of events, you'll want to avoid any suggestion to the contrary. That means you need to be careful to avoid "thanking" a news reporter for "publicity," which suggests that reporter is somehow doing you a favor by highlighting you or your enterprise. Rather, it would be more appropriate to tell a reporter you're pleased to see that the newspaper, magazine, or broadcast thought this was an important topic to cover.

After you've received news coverage, follow-up notes are very uncommon, but if you feel compelled to send a note, you might simply say you thought the reporter, or interviewer, did a good job with the subject, and that you thought the article or program was very interesting. This is your opportunity to tell the newsperson that his or her work was noticed. If you have had any audience feedback, mention it to the reporter; that information is more flattering than any praise you can offer.

However, if you should ever be a guest on an *entertainment* program rather than a news program, it is always acceptable to send a note of appreciation. Address it to the producer and the staff. Again, be sure to mention any positive response you've had.

3. Don't become a pest

Ask reporters what bothers them most, and many will say it's people who are constantly nagging them for coverage. No one, and no organization, can be *that* newsworthy. Therefore, it makes no sense to deluge the media with daily press releases, or even weekly ones. You only diminish the impact.

As a general rule, avoid sending more than one press release every two or three months to any individual media outlet.

c. PYRAMID ON PREVIOUS PUBLICITY

It is important, when organizing a publicity plan, to allow for flexibility so that you can respond immediately to any positive results. If, for instance, one of your press releases should earn you a favorable feature story in a small "shopper" newspaper, don't leave it at that. Take the time to parlay that attention into even more publicity.

This kind of effort is called "pyramiding" on your publicity success. It provides the means to build systematically on your publicity achievements by using one media mention to motivate interest elsewhere. Pyramiding allows you to prove your "newsworthiness" by demonstrating that other media outlets have found you worthy of coverage. By clipping and saving all of your press mentions and keeping a record of your broadcast interviews and Internet appearances, you will have a tangible history of your coverage to present to new media outlets.

Pyramiding offers double value to any publicity program. In the short term, immediately following any successful publicity coup — such as a feature article in a trade journal highlighting your company — you can notify other media for a possible follow-up story. In the long term, perhaps after a year or two of periodic coverage by your local media, you can use your accumulated clippings to generate interest in the national media.

When pyramiding on publicity in this fashion, a few guidelines will help ensure your success.

It is important to keep your name in the news so that both the public and the members of the media remember your name. This can lead to further publicity opportunities.

1. Crossing over

If you are ever the subject of favorable treatment in one medium, such as a newspaper, use that mention to generate coverage in some other medium like radio or television. For example, if your new business is featured in a weekly community-oriented newspaper, don't send the clipping to a similar publication. Instead, send it — along with a cover letter and press kit — to a local radio or television outlet. Although many journalists do look for story ideas in material that has already been published or broadcast, most of them prefer to be the first to cover a story in their particular medium.

To put it another way, you stand a better chance of pyramiding a newspaper story into a radio interview than you do of using a clipping from one newspaper to gain mention in a different newspaper. Likewise, once you have been interviewed on radio, you can send a press release to a newspaper describing your radio experience.

2. Local to national or national to local

To attract wider media attention, you can send your media kit enclosing copies of local press interviews to regional and national magazines and TV shows asking the recipients if they might be interested in a related story. If you have appeared on television or spoken on the radio before, be sure to mention that in your cover letter.

By the same token, if your first mention in the media should come in a nationwide broadcast or publication, you can send that information to your local media either in a press release or a media kit. Include a cover letter explaining that you have already received national attention for your work and asking if they would like to know more about you.

3. Snowball effect

For publicity purposes, it is important to keep your name in the news so that both the public and members of the media remember your name. Therefore, even if your initial publicity efforts produce only a modest response, pyramiding can be very important to achieving media success. By knowing how to start the snowball of publicity rolling in the first place, you can create an avalanche of attention.

d. WATCH YOUR TIMING

How does the evening newscast manage to get everything covered in exactly the same number of minutes every night? Why is the Monday morning paper always filled with articles even though nothing really "newsworthy" usually happens on Sundays? Where do talk shows always find the perfect guest for every topic? Is it just luck? Of course not: it's planning.

Understanding how, when, and why each medium makes its planning decisions will give you a better chance of getting your story on their agenda. And making note of such information in your media list will help you score higher when you mail your messages.

1. The three-cycle rule

When your press release is linked to a specific time, date, or event you should schedule it to reach its destination at least three editions, broadcasts, or publications in advance. That means if you're notifying weekly papers — or a weekly feature in a daily paper — about an event, they usually need to know about three weeks ahead.

When contacting a television station for coverage in a daily newscast, your best chance is to get your news release to them three days ahead of time.

By the same rule, a monthly magazine needs your information at least three months prior to publication, although holiday and special issues are sometimes planned as much as a year in advance of publication.

Editors can sometimes arrange coverage of a story at the last minute, but that's an effort they save for compelling late-breaking news only.

2. When timing is of no importance

On the other hand, there are those times when your news release is not specifically tied to a certain time or related to a particular date. When you are sending out a consumer hint as a way to get your name in the news, for example, the publication date is not of utmost importance. Even in that case, however, it is still best to get it into everyone's hands at the same time. That way, when an editor looks over your information, he or she hasn't already seen it in the morning paper or heard it on last night's news report.

e. TAKE ADVANTAGE OF A "PHOTO OP"

Occasionally an event that is not newsworthy by itself will get media coverage simply because the occasion offers an unusual or exciting photographic opportunity, known as a "photo op." If, for example, your community group held its annual luncheon at a hotel, it would not be a major news event. But if you invited an ice sculptor to prepare the centerpiece and then notified the press that this talented artist would be creating his work before their very eyes, the media would probably be there to capture the action on film and videotape.

That is a photo op — no news, just visuals. But the value is that by using those photographs, the media will also mention that the ice sculpture demonstration was part of your community group's annual luncheon.

If you are planning a photographic opportunity and the event is open to the public, you can send a press release. Or, if you only want to notify the media, you can send a media advisory, as explained later in this chapter under the heading "Holding a News Conference."

f. USE PUBLIC SERVICE ANNOUNCEMENTS

One advanced publicity technique you might want to use one day is the public service announcement, commonly referred to as a "PSA." Public service announcements are statements designed for radio and television broadcast and aimed at informing the public about some issue of general interest. For example, the government uses PSAs to broadcast brief tax-preparation tips and reminders just before the deadline for paying annual income taxes.

Even though PSAs must be free of commercial content, entrepreneurs are learning to take advantage of them by occasionally providing helpful services to the public and having it announced over radio and TV. Sponsoring fingerprinting days for children, fire department demonstrations of home safety techniques, or displays of burglar-proofing equipment are examples of this type of public service activity.

PSAs fit into their own special niche in the media. Although they're not quite news stories and they're definitely not advertisements, they can be valuable as publicity.

1. Radio versus television

PSAs are scheduled for the convenience of the broadcasters. The statements are used to fill odd moments of time, such as a few seconds between commercials. At radio stations, announcers read PSAs over the air either live or on tape. On television, however, PSAs must be "produced," which requires time and trouble on the part of the station. Your chances of coverage on the radio are much greater, therefore, than they are on television.

In any case, to inquire about placing a PSA, you need to call your local station and get the name of the individual in the public affairs department who handles public service announcements. But before you place the call, you should understand the limits imposed by the media. On the radio an average PSA lasts approximately 10 to 20 seconds. On television, the typical length is 30 seconds.

2. Writing the PSA release

Although a public service announcement is similar to a press release, a few of the rules for writing them are different. Note the following differences in particular:

It is generally easier to get your public service announcement aired on the radio than on television.

(a) Deadline: Submit PSAs at least two weeks in advance of the desired broadcast date to allow the TV or radio station the time needed to pre-record it for broadcast.

(b) Release date: Instead of providing a release date, type the exact dates on which your announcement may be read on the air.

(c) Special instructions: Since broadcast announcers are not familiar with your organization, provide (in parentheses) the phonetic pronunciation of any unusual, foreign, or difficult-to-pronounce words or names.

(d) Media kit: Sending your PSA in a media kit can sometimes help to convince the recipient that not only does your event deserve a free announcement, it is also worthy of an in-depth story.

See Samples 19 and 20 for examples of releases for PSAs.

g. HOLD A NEWS CONFERENCE

If you suddenly find yourself with a story that's generating a great deal of public interest, would you know how to handle it? One of the

PHREDD'S PHARMACY

4321 CAPSULE COURT
PHREDERICK, MARYLAND 00000
Telephone: (555) 555-5555
Fax: (555) 555-1111
E-mail: phredd@pharmacy.com

Public Service Announcement

START: December 1, 20—

DISCONTINUE: December 15, 20—

CONTACT: Philomena Phredd

  Days: (555) 555-5555

  Evenings: (555) 555-1212

20 Seconds

When you think of the upcoming holidays, consider those children who won't be receiving any gifts this year.

Phredd's Pharmacy, at 4321 Capsule Court in Phrederick, Maryland, is collecting new toys to distribute to youngsters who otherwise would face a very bleak holiday season.

Please bring in your donations before December fifteenth.

The children thank you.

PHREDD'S PHARMACY

4321 CAPSULE COURT
PHREDERICK, MARYLAND 00000
Telephone: (555) 555-5555
Fax: (555) 555-1111
E-mail: phredd@pharmacy.com

Public Service Announcement

START: December 1, 20—

DISCONTINUE: December 15, 20—

CONTACT: Philomena Phredd

Days: (555) 555-5555

Evenings: (555) 555-1212

10 Seconds

Phredd's Pharmacy, at 4321 Capsule Court in Phrederick, Maryland, is collecting new toys for needy children this holiday season. Please make your donation before December fifteenth.

best ways is to arrange a news conference, also referred to as a press conference.

Designed to allow you to speak to several members of the media at once, a news conference not only results in wider coverage, it also saves you the time and effort of repeated one-on-one interviews with reporters.

But press conferences are not for everyone. It's important to know when a news conference is appropriate and when it is not.

1. Purpose

When you call a news conference, you're telling editors and producers that there is a specific time set aside for the coverage of your announcement.

2. Subject matter

The media needs a compelling reason to send a reporter or a photographer to a news conference. What kinds of topics interest them?

(a) A well-known person who is otherwise inaccessible to reporters

(b) The findings of a recent study or project with widespread public interest

(c) A significant development in a story that has already been receiving attention

(d) A response to multiple media queries for information

3. Notifying the media

To let the media know you're holding a news conference, you should send out a special notice called a media advisory, or press advisory as it is also known. Invite both print and broadcast outlets by sending the advisory to the appropriate names on your media mailing list, including the local assignment desk of any wire service in your area for inclusion in the daybook.

A media advisory is basically nothing more than a specialized invitation to reporters. In style and content it differs from a press release because the media advisory doesn't provide the actual news story, just information on the press conference. Not intended to be printed in the newspaper or broadcast over the air, the media advisory is strictly to invite the media to attend the planned event.

Written like a memorandum, it should be typed, single spaced, and include five basic items of information regarding the scheduled news conference: who, what, when, where, and background information. See Sample 21 for an example of a typical media advisory.

If you happen to have an item of "breaking news" — something major that has happened suddenly — and you're sure there is substantial interest, it is acceptable to call a news conference the same day by notifying all your media contacts, either by fax or over the telephone. It's a bit more risky to do so, though, as reporters might not be available to attend.

4.   Scheduling for local television news

If your goal in scheduling a news conference is to have your story appear on that day's local television news programs, you need to be familiar with newsroom headlines. On average, to receive the most coverage on weekdays, plan your press conference for mid morning. Even an early afternoon news conference will draw some attention if it allows reporters enough time to put together a story for that evening's newscast. But any news conference scheduled after 3:30 p.m. is automatically less likely to get coverage because deadline pressures build as the day goes on.

What day is best for television coverage? Being flexible can mean a media coup. Weekends are generally very slow times in newsrooms, so scheduling your news conference on Sunday can mean more prominent coverage.

5.   Elements of a news conference

There are three basic components of a news conference:

(a) A "handout" consisting of a news release or media kit given to reporters just before the press conference

(b) A statement made by the organization's spokesperson including a few minutes of background, history, details, and explanation

(c) A question-and-answer session to fill the rest of the allotted time

Be sure to be sensitive to media deadlines when scheduling a news conference. By holding your conference in the morning, you give reporters enough time to put together a story before the deadline.

HOMETOWN SYMPHONY ORCHESTRA
345 CHORAL WAY
HOMETOWN, NEW YORK 00000

MEDIA ADVISORY

Contact: Victor Vibrato
                    Telephone: (555) 555-5555
                    Fax: (555) 555-1111
                    www.hometownsymphony.org

WHAT: News conference to announce future plans of the Hometown Symphony Or-
                    chestra as a result of fundraising efforts.

WHEN: Tuesday, January 12, 20—, 11:30 a.m.

WHERE: Symphony Hall Rehearsal Studio, 345 Choral Way, Hometown, New York

WHO: Victor Vibrato, Concertmaster

BACKGROUND: The Hometown Symphony Orchestra has experienced financial difficulties over a
                    seven-year period. Last March, the Friends of the Symphony launched a
                    fundraising drive with a goal of $50,000. This news conference will reveal the re-
                    sults of that effort.

6.   Visuals

If real estate depends on "location, location, location," then television needs "visuals, visuals, visuals." Because displays and demonstrations are more attention-getting than "talking heads," you can increase your chance of coverage on all the media by incorporating some type of visual aid into your presentation.

As a rule of thumb, at a news conference, if one speaker out of twelve makes use of a prop, that person will be the one who is shown on the evening news and featured in the newspaper photograph.

Not all visual aids are a plus, however. Stay away from slides and overhead projectors because they tend to slow down the pace and darken the room too much for photographs. Instead, aim for a display or prop that puts you in the picture as well.

7.   The setup

In order to flow smoothly and comfortably, a press conference should be set up in advance and include the following items:

- ◆   Head table for the speaker(s)
- ◆   Chairs for reporters
- ◆   Space behind the chairs for TV tripods
- ◆   Electrical outlets for camera lights

Two optional items you might want to include are a podium for the speaker and simple refreshments for the press, such as coffee and doughnuts.

8.   The 5- and 30-minute rules

It's crucial that you be organized and on time, and that your entire presentation, and question-answer time, is kept within 30 minutes. Reporters simply won't tolerate a long lecture from you about every single detail, and their news stories can only hit the key points. So a good rule of thumb is that no individual should speak for more than five minutes. The purpose of a press conference, after all, is to give reporters the opportunity to ask questions. Some reporters might wish to delve into more detail, and might want to talk with your further at the end of the news conference. Make yourself accessible for those follow-ups, but allow the other news people to leave.

A news conference is not an event for beginners. A failure at this level could damage your credibility, so make sure you're ready before you act.

9. Avoid overreaching

A news conference is not an event for beginners. It requires a newsworthy topic, organization, and polished presentation. You'll want to have some experience dealing with reporters before setting up such an event, because a failure at this level could damage your credibility.

h. INCLUDE THE INTERNET

Shortly after its inception, the Internet quickly became a prime target for publicity campaigns. After all, not only is the World Wide Web accessible internationally, but many of the promotional opportunities it offers cost absolutely nothing. So whether you're designing a publicity blitz for your organization or yourself, be sure to integrate the Internet into your plans.

Of course, as with all bids for media attention, the type of outreach you choose will depend on what you're promoting. But the following section should give you several ideas for making the most of your Internet options.

1. E-send your message

If you're already sending your own original e-newsletter to regular customers and potential clients, consider adding selected media recipients to your mailing list. When you're sure your personal periodical is brief, newsworthy and well-written, target a few of your favorite editors or reporters. One Web site operator who did this was rewarded when a major publishing house offered to turn several of her newsletters into a book, simply because one of its editors had enjoyed reading the short articles.

2. Talk it up

Love to answer questions? Perhaps you're the perfect candidate to get free publicity on the Internet as an online chat guest. Visit a variety of Internet chats before you offer your own expertise so you'll be familiar with the different formats that are used. For example, some chats are live, while others consist of questions which are answered days in advance of the posted interview date. At some Web sites the interviewee is required to type his or her own answers, while at others the host handles all the computer interaction from a remote location.

In any case, being a chat guest on a heavily visited Web site can boost your business or heighten awareness of your cause. Just be sure to use proper "Netiquette" and ask in advance if you can announce your own Web site address during the chat or if the host will do it for you. And always remember to send out news releases in advance of your appearance in order to garner the largest possible audience.

3. Web publishing

Dream of becoming a published writer? One woman began a lucrative career as a columnist by posting original business hints on her own Web site. Before long, she was offered a salary to contribute a column of similar helpful hints to an online magazine aimed at entrepreneurs. How did the woman make sure the e-magazine knew about her Web site? Every month when she posted new tips, she sent a press release to the magazine's editor.

Just as you might offer to write an article for a newspaper or magazine, you can also try to publish a freelance piece in an online magazine. Simply approach the editor in exactly the same way you would for a regular magazine. You might not get paid, but it would be an opportunity to reach a new audience without paying for advertising. Just be sure to include your Web site address as a reference for readers.

4. On-camera options

Want to be on TV? Visit the Web site of those talk shows or news programs that you think would best showcase your particular product or service. Read the content thoroughly, then use the e-mail address provided to contact the correct person and suggest yourself as a guest. Try to post a message which states your case in no more than two or three paragraphs, then include your own phone number and Internet address. Many such Web sites even post upcoming program titles and invite visitors to apply for guest appearances.

5. Increase visibility

In order to facilitate the media's choosing you as an interview subject, list your Web address in as many online Internet directories as possible. Many such listings are free of charge and they can help turn your Web site into a goldmine of publicity possibilities. And if you have a physical location in addition to your virtual address, consider including that on your Web page as well, as your location can sometimes make you a more desirable subject for interviewers.

6. Post your opinions

In the same way you can write letters to the editor and sign your company name, you can post informational or newsworthy messages to newsgroups or forums on the Internet. They should show your professionalism and expertise, as well as provide a way for readers to contact you and your organization.

7. Add online interactions

Online giveaways, like in-store raffles, provide a good way to attract the media's attention and generate interest in your cause.

With a Web site, it's easy to send something by e-mail to anyone who requests it. One company, for instance, provides free advice on buying new tires, while a another offers a price comparison list for computer upgrades. In another case, a corporate trainer who specializes in curing office chaos conducts a monthly contest on his Web site and awards actual prizes.

Just remember — when you plan an Internet event, send announcements to the media and you can increase your audience exponentially.

8. Make connections

Instant links from one Web site to another are very helpful, both to customers and media. Spend some time becoming familiar with any Web sites to which you think you might want to be linked, then contact them and inquire about creating such an arrangement.

Sometimes links are best when made between non-competing sites, and other times the best links are simply a long list of similar sites. In some cases, perhaps you could barter a business service for a link or maybe you'd rather offer someone a link from your site in exchange for one from theirs. In any case, as one consultant has said, "Every link means more people know about my business."

9. Electronic media kit

Some creative Web designers include an entire section just for the media on their Internet sites, where complete press kits can be downloaded,

The more links your Web site has, the more people know about you. Try to convince other Web sites to include a link to your own site, perhaps in exchange for a link to their site on your Web site.

including photographs, text, and even video. If you'd like to incorporate this feature into your own Web site it would be wise to find out how most media recipients would want the material formatted, and how large a file they expect for pictures and video. In any case, you should always post one or two of your most recent press releases for everyone who visits your site, especially the media.

i. PRACTICE DAMAGE CONTROL

One of the most advanced publicity strategies is a technique known as "damage control," a process designed to turn a negative situation into a positive one through media publicity. If you — or the industry in which you're involved — should ever receive unflattering or unfavorable public attention, you can learn to turn that adversity into advantage through damage control techniques.

Basically, there are four rules for overcoming obstacles and minimizing damage whenever an unfortunate situation arises.

1. Make yourself accessible to the press

Every reporter knows there are two sides to every story, and sometimes even more. But if the media can't reach you to hear your side, it might appear as if you are trying to hide something. The headline "Business Owner Refuses Comment" creates a negative impression, so if journalists are calling, take the time to talk to them.

2. Show concern

Showing that you care about the situation, and the people affected, is a good way to win the public's understanding.

3. Take positive action

What can you or your company do to improve the situation? Make it clear that you want to help in some way.

4. Keep it short

Whether you're talking to one reporter or addressing a room filled with journalists, open your remarks by saying that you have only a few minutes. That way you can excuse yourself if you become uncomfortable with hostile questions that put you on the defensive.

j. VIDEO NEWS RELEASES

Another advanced promotional tool is the video news release. Definitely not a do-it-yourself project, the video news release is a sophisticated method of generating media attention. It requires the expertise of a professional electronic news gathering camera crew, an experienced producer, and a well-equipped production facility.

Specifically, a video news release, known in the industry as a VNR, is a video-taped production intended for national distribution. The subject pays all production costs and offers the VNR free to TV outlets: bureaus, stations, and networks. Usually, this involves expensive forms of transmission, such as satellite feeds.

A video news release is *not* the same as a promotional tape or a company sales message. To get on the air it must be timely and focus on a newsworthy topic. Examples of suitable subjects include technological breakthroughs, celebrity events, and health or medical reports of widespread interest. If you are interested in pursuing publicity through the use of a video news release, contact established companies and compare cost estimates and services provided. Generally, the minimum price for a VNR is more than $10,000.

k. ADD TO YOUR PUBLICITY PLANNER

When you first created your Publicity Planner, you labelled a file for "Clippings and quotes" and another for "Industry news." Both these files will serve as resources when you launch your pyramiding efforts.

And now you can add three more file folders for your advanced publicity attempts. Label these "Media advisories" for your press conference and photo op announcements; "Correspondence" for any personal notes you send to members of the media; and "PSAs" to store permanent copies of any public service announcements you send.

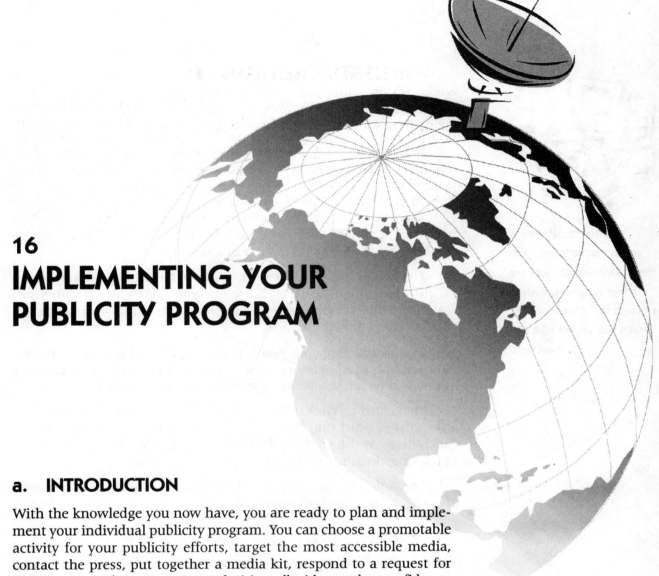

16
IMPLEMENTING YOUR PUBLICITY PROGRAM

a. INTRODUCTION

With the knowledge you now have, you are ready to plan and implement your individual publicity program. You can choose a promotable activity for your publicity efforts, target the most accessible media, contact the press, put together a media kit, respond to a request for an interview, and even appear on television, all with complete confidence.

In this chapter you will learn about the final ingredient: how to estimate the cost of your publicity campaign. Following that, you will review the steps for setting up a publicity plan from start to finish. A section on scheduling will explain the need for flexibility. And finally, a case study will show you the form your final plan might take.

b. WORK OUT A BUDGET

Publicity is sometimes referred to as "free advertising" because the media coverage is given away at no cost. Nevertheless, there are a few

Although publicity is sometimes referred to as "free advertising," there are minor expenses, such as postage and photocopying, which you should take into account.

expenses incurred during the publicity process. Although the basic tools are the same items needed for running any business — stationery, file folders, and business cards — you should set aside a certain amount of money for promotional expenses.

Before you can decide how much money you will be spending, however, you need to begin by getting out your Publicity Planning calendar and penciling in one promotable event each month for which you can send press releases to at least a few media outlets. If you want to start out easily, aim for simple announcements, such as the anniversary of your organization's founding, your election to a club office, or your participation in a seminar.

Then, once or twice a year, plan to participate in something slightly more high profile — like holding an open house at your headquarters with balloons, refreshments, and free tours — for which you can send out a media kit.

Decide which of your publicity efforts will be fairly small, involving sending press releases to only ten or twelve media targets at a time, and which you want to spend more time preparing.

Then turn to Worksheet 5 and begin to estimate your costs. Notice, it is divided into two sections: a one-time expense section for such items as the Publicity Planner filing system and a monthly section for estimating your expenses for each mailing.

The following list will provide you with some additional guidelines regarding your expected expenses.

1.   Postage

The cost for your postage will depend strictly on how many press releases and media kits you send and how often you send them. A good guideline for press releases is once a month or every other month. If, for example, your goal is to mail one press release a month to twenty different media outlets, calculate the amount you will need for postage. If you also plan to mail media kits each year, remember to allow additional postage for more weight.

2.   Photocopying

Estimate how many copies you will need on a monthly or yearly basis and then calculate the cost.

WORKSHEET 5
PUBLICITY BUDGET

1. Publicity Planner

   Item   **Estimated cost**

   Calendar   _____

   File system   _____

   File folders and labels   _____

   Media kit folders and labels   _____

   Media list system   _____

   Printing: Business cards   _____

                     Personalized Rolodex cards   _____

                     Stationery   _____

   Other _____   _____

2. Each mailing

   Item   **Estimated cost**

   Brochures   _____

   Envelopes   _____

   Paper and copying charges   _____

   Photographs/photographer fees   _____

   Postage   _____

   Other _____   _____

3. Photographs

If you plan to hire a professional photographer for your publicity photos, get estimates from a variety of sources. Usually the more copies of a picture you order, the less expensive it is for each copy. If you do it yourself, remember to include any film and developing costs.

4. Media kit covers

Before purchasing media kit covers, you might find it is less expensive to buy in volume. Check with a variety of vendors before settling on a style and color.

c. REVIEW YOUR PUBLICITY PLANS

Publicity is an invaluable tool in promoting any endeavor. But working within a structured system will give you a better chance of success. Before you actually draw up your publicity plan, review the steps necessary for setting up your Publicity Planner and implementing your program.

1. Putting together a Publicity Planner

It is essential to begin your quest for media attention by setting up a filing system strictly for your publicity purposes. Remember, the Publicity Planner incorporates two aspects: a place and a plan.

Analyze your requirements and then set up a filing system that you will find convenient, either permanent or portable. Purchase your file folders, label them, and begin to file relevant material. Following is a suggested list of file names:

- Biography
- Brochures
- Business cards
- Clippings and quotes
- Community events
- Correspondence
- Fact sheet
- Industry news

- Interview notes
- Letters from customers
- Media advisories
- Media kit folders
- Media kit labels
- Media list
- New product release
- Press releases sent
- Promotion ideas
- Public service announcements
- Publicity photos
- Public speaking/teaching
- Published writing
- Stationery
- Suggested questions
- Writing opportunities

2.   Choosing an activity

Review section **e. Fifty Perfectly Promotable Ideas** in chapter 3 and think about the kinds of events you might like to promote.

Consider charities, community organizations, volunteer services, public speaking, and other activities before you decide which direction you'd like to take.

At this time it's not necessary to commit yourself to one particular idea, but you should begin to pinpoint where your interests lie.

3.   Compiling a media list

Set up a telephone-address system for storing your media contact list. Choose index cards, a Rolodex, or a computer-based file, but be sure to maintain it separately from your customer mailing list.

Unlike advertising, publicity is limited by what the media decides, not what you decide. Therefore, you might have to make changes in your plan as you go along in order to achieve it.

Follow the guidelines on Worksheet 4 in chapter 9 for compiling the information necessary for your list.

4. Drawing up a plan

Get out your calendar, look through your Publicity Planner file marked "Community events," and begin to formulate an idea for one promotable activity every month. Write down your various options (in pencil) on your calendar.

Then, once you decide on the date of the event you are going to promote, you must work backward and fill in the following:

(a) The date you plan to write the press release

(b) The date you will assemble the media kits if necessary

(c) The date you will mail the material to the media, keeping in mind the various deadlines

5. Getting started

Choose one idea for your first publicity effort and set the date for mailing your first news release. Remember, if you have never practiced publicity before you will probably prefer to test the waters by starting with a simple promotion and an easily accessible media target.

Just make sure you allow enough time to plan it, to prepare your news releases, to assemble your materials, and to mail everything to the media in time for publication or broadcast.

6. Scheduling

Just as pilots file a flight plan before every trip, you need a clear picture of where you're headed with your publicity program. But your blueprint, which will chart the course of your entire campaign, should be flexible enough to allow for mid-course corrections along the way.

With publicity you can't control the actual outcome of your efforts. Unlike advertising, where you can choose your medium and control your message, publicity is limited by what the media decides, not what you decide. Therefore, although you know where you want to go, you might have to make changes in your plan as you go along in order to get there.

That's another reason why having a Publicity Planner is so important. When you need to change your plans or find another way to generate attention, you can turn to your files and find a variety of ideas at your fingertips.

For best results, plan to participate in no more than one promotional activity every month, and no less than one every two months. Make press releases part of your regular program, and anticipate sending out media kits once or twice a year. Then, as you begin to see the results of your efforts, update your planning calendar from time to time to make sure your planned activities are still relevant to the coverage you're receiving.

d. A ONE-YEAR PUBLICITY PLAN CASE STUDY

To help you get started with your own publicity program, the samples on the following pages outline the publicity procedure of a small business owner in the first year of business.

Once you have read the case study outlined in Sample 22 and the sample press releases sent out by Tom Talker (Samples 23 through 28), you'll be ready to sit down and work out your own strategy for success.

SAMPLE 22
NEW BUSINESS CASE STUDY:
TALK OF THE TOWN TELEPHONE STORE

July

Store owner, Tom Talker, announces the store's grand opening with a press release to local newspapers, radio stations, and TV stations. (See Sample 23.)

Result: The daily newspaper sends a photographer to get a picture of Tom Talker with a cartoon phone. It appears in the "Features" section, with a caption about Tom's new store. Also, a reporter from a weekly newspaper calls and interviews Tom over the phone, resulting in a short article in the business pages.

August

Tom Talker decides to ride the coattails of a national event by relating his product to the annual fall migration of college students to campuses all across the country. (See Sample 24.)

Result: A local TV station does a news story about sending youngsters to college, and includes a shot of the telephone alarm clock, saying "Here at Talk of the Town telephone store, the owner recommends sending this model off to school with freshmen who want to be sure they get to those early classes on time."

In addition, a local radio station rewrites Tom's press release slightly, and reads it on the air several times.

October

To keep his name in the news, Tom Talker ties his telephone store into American Thanksgiving by co-sponsoring an event with another local business. A press release is sent to local and regional newspapers, radio stations, and television stations. (See Sample 25.)

Result: Many of the daily and weekly newspapers print a version of Tom's press release, and he gives away 400 copies of the recipes, each emblazoned with his store logo.

December

Tom Talker sends a press release to the media with advice for last-minute holiday shoppers. (See Sample 26.)

Result: No local media follow up the press release. Tom Talker makes a note in his calendar to contact the press by early November next year to become part of the media's holiday shopping coverage.

February

By looking at an almanac, Tom Talker discovers that this month includes "National Hearing Week" and recognizes an opportunity to help out his community. After making the necessary arrangements, he donates a Telephone Device for the Deaf to his local library and issues press releases. (See Sample 27.)

Result: Tom Talker's picture appears on the front page of his weekly paper, along with a long article featuring quotes from local residents praising Talker's generosity.

April

Tom Talker, in his ongoing contacts with the local Board of Business, hears of an upcoming seminar for people starting small businesses. He offers to lead a workshop on the selection of business telephone equipment. He sends a press release. (See Sample 28.)

Result: Although a local newspaper calls Tom to verify the time and place of his workshop, no reporters show up that evening. Apparently other news developments have drawn the media's attention. But, as with all his publicity efforts, Tom is pleased with the experience he gained from participating in the event. He writes down the best questions from the group and adds them to his "Promotion ideas" folder for a possible pamphlet. He does plan to try again at a later date, this time in his own store.

TALK OF THE TOWN

123 CENTERVILLE MALL
CENTERVILLE, DAKOTA 00000
Telephone: (555) 555-5555
Fax: (555) 555-1111
www.talkofthetown.com

PRESS RELEASE

July 1, 20—   Contact: Tom Talker
For Immediate Release   Daytime: (555) 555-5555
                                                     Evening: (555) 555-1212

New Store Features Novelty Telephones

Beginning Thursday, July 25, 20—, at 10 a.m., fans of cartoon shows will be able to talk directly with their favorite characters — or rather through their favorite characters turned into telephones. When owner Tom Talker opens the doors to his shop in Centerville Mall it will mark the end of more than three years of planning.

"I plan to stock novelty telephones of every sort," he said. "My own house is overflowing with unusual phones I've collected all my life." Mr. Talker said he ordered a large supply of one unusual phone, sculpted to resemble a kitten. "I expect that to be the one cat lovers will go to first," he said.

-more-

Telephone

2

The new store, which will be open Mondays through Saturdays from 10 a.m. to 8 p.m., will also feature a service center where customers can bring in any phone for repair or reconditioning.

For further information, call (555) 555-5555 or visit the store's Web site at www.talkofthetown.com.

-end-

TALK OF THE TOWN

123 CENTERVILLE MALL
CENTERVILLE, DAKOTA 00000
Telephone: (555) 555-5555
Fax: (555) 555-1111
www.talkofthetown.com

PRESS RELEASE

August 1, 20—
For Immediate Release

Contact: Tom Talker
Daytime: (555) 555-5555
Evening: (555) 555-1212

College-Bound? Don't Forget the Phone Batteries!

A local telephone store owner is reminding parents of college-bound students to send their new freshmen off with a fresh battery for their wireless phone. "It's a hectic time, and this is one way parents can help their kids stay in touch," said Tom Talker, owner of Talk of the Town store. "Today's batteries last twice as long as the older ones. That means your student should have enough talk time to get through the whole school year without a problem."

The newest trend for students, according to Mr. Talker, is the telephone alarm clock. "It's a real space-saver for the dorm rooms," he says.

-more-

Telephones

2

The Talk of the Town, located in Centerville Mall, opened last month. The shop features 275 different designs, including four styles of the telephone alarm clock.

For more information, call (555) 555-5555 or visit the Web site at www.talkofthetown.com.

-end-

TALK OF THE TOWN

123 CENTERVILLE MALL
CENTERVILLE, DAKOTA 00000
Telephone: (555) 555-5555
Fax: (555) 555-1111
www.talkofthetown.com

PRESS RELEASE

October 30, 20—   Contact: Tom Talker
For Immediate Release   Daytime: (555) 555-5555
                                                          Evening: (555) 555-1212

Talking Turkey — Telephone Help for Cooks

A local businessman has teamed up with one of the area's best-known chefs to offer Thanksgiving cooking help in ten telephone and web lessons. Would-be cooks can hear a blue-ribbon recipe and cooking hints in pre-recorded lessons, available through Thanksgiving Day by calling a special phone number, (555) 555-8888, or by visiting the website at www.talkof-thetown.com/turkey.

The cooking instructions are being made available through two local business owners in Centerville, Dakota — Tom Talker, owner of Talk of the Town telephone shop, and Charlotte Cuisine, head chef at Chez Cuisine restaurant. "You don't have to call up your Aunt Millie and ask her how to make chestnut dressing step by step. You can hear how Chef Cuisine does it," Mr. Talker said.

-more-

Cooking

2

The dial-up cooking lessons are concise and include such hints as "Stuffing Made Simple," and "Fifteen-Minute Apple Pie." Taste samples of the most popular recipes will be offered at Talk of the Town and Chez Cuisine through Thanksgiving. For further information, call (555) 555-5555 or visit the Web site at www.talkofthetown.com/turkey.

-end-

TALK OF THE TOWN

123 CENTERVILLE MALL
CENTERVILLE, DAKOTA 00000
Telephone: (555) 555-5555
Fax: (555) 555-1111
www.talkofthetown.com

PRESS RELEASE

December 1, 20—
For Immediate Release

Contact: Tom Talker
Daytime: (555) 555-5555
Evening: (555) 555-1212

Holiday Gift Craze: Robot Telephones

When you're holiday shopping, what do you give the person who already has everything? The trend at one of Centerville's newest stores is robot telephones.

"I can't believe it," said Tom Talker, owner of Talk of the Town store in Centerville Mall. "I've reordered four times just to keep up with the demand."

Mr. Talker noted that the industry-wide lowering of prices has made robot phones more affordable for more people. "It used to be something that most people only dreamed of — having a walking, talking telephone to handle your calls for you. Now that it's really here, everybody wants one," he said.

-more-

Robot

2

Mr. Talker already has a waiting list two pages long of people who want to buy robot telephones as holiday gifts. And he warned shoppers not to wait until the last minute; his deadline for the last order of the year is December 20, 20—.

Last year, fewer than 2,000 robot telephones were sold, according to an industry survey. Talker predicts that "by the end of the next decade, every household will have a robot telephone."

For more information, contact Tom Talker at (555) 555-5555 or visit the Web site at www.talkofthetown.com.

-end-

TALK OF THE TOWN

123 CENTERVILLE MALL
CENTERVILLE, DAKOTA 00000
Telephone: (555) 555-5555
Fax: (555) 555-1111
www.talkofthetown.com

PRESS RELEASE

February 1, 20—
For Immediate Release

Contact: Tom Talker
Daytime: (555) 555-5555
Evening: (555) 555-1212

Hearing Week Means Help from Local Business Owner

The Centerville Community Library now has equipment to aid the hearing-impaired thanks to a recent donation from local business owner Tom Talker. The proprietor of Talk of the Town telephone mall in Centerville Mall, Mr. Talker has presented the library with a Telephone Device for the Deaf.

Centerville librarian Barry Books said he has wanted the equipment for a long time, but no money was available for the purchase. When Mr. Talker learned of the library's need, he made arrangements to donate the equipment in honor of National Hearing Week.

-more-

Donation

2

"I am so pleased to be able to contribute this much-needed machine for the use of our residents," Mr. Talker said. "And I hope to be able to make additional donations each year for this worthwhile cause."

Mr. Talker said the special telephone can be used by anyone who has a similar device in his or her home. He estimated the cost of the equipment at $500. "But the money means nothing compared with the value to our citizens," he added.

-end-

TALK OF THE TOWN

123 CENTERVILLE MALL
CENTERVILLE, DAKOTA 00000
Telephone: (555) 555-5555
Fax: (555) 555-1111
www.talkofthetown.com

PRESS RELEASE

April 2, 20—   Contact: Tom Talker
For Immediate Release   Daytime: (555) 555-5555
                                                        Evening: (555) 555-1212

Calling In Profits: Phone Advice for Entrepreneurs

The right telephone equipment can make or break a new business. What type of service is best for data transmission? What kind of Internet access does this business need? Voice mail or a live operator?

"These are just some of the things to consider when launching a new enterprise," says Tom Talker, owner of the Talk of the Town phone store. Mr. Talker is offering a special seminar to help entrepreneurs learn more about today's options in communications. The free event is scheduled for 7:00 p.m. Thursday, April 20, in the Centerville Auditorium.

Mr. Talker, whose telephone store opened one year ago in the Centerville Mall, has compiled a list of helpful hints for new businesses which will be available to seminar participants at no charge.

For reservations and further information, contact Tom Talker at (555) 555-5555 or visit the Web site at www.talkofthetown.com.

-end-

17
ANSWERING THE MOST FREQUENTLY ASKED QUESTIONS

a. INTRODUCTION

Once you've been practicing your publicity skills for a while, a few questions will undoubtedly arise. Although the publicity process itself is easy to implement, you might occasionally run into situations which don't go as smoothly as you expect. To help you solve your problems, the following section provides answers to the questions most people ask.

b. QUESTIONS AND ANSWERS

Q. Can we invite reporters for an "educational" tour of our facility so they can learn about the work we do? That way they'd understand why we deserve more coverage in the media.

To make your mark in the media, simply send a substantive letter or news release once a month. It doesn't have to take up a lot of your time and money to get publicity.

A. No. Journalists are paid to keep the public informed of "newsworthy" happenings, not to spend their time studying every organization in town. Send invitations only when you're holding a noteworthy event and you'll gain the respect of reporters.

Q. I don't have the time (or the money) to stage a major promotional activity every month. Can I still plan an effective publicity campaign?

A. Yes. To make your mark in the media, simply send a substantive letter or news release once a month. For example, you can write to the editor of a newspaper or magazine, comment on a recent story, and sign your name along with the name of your business or non-profit group. Or send a press release announcing your employee or volunteer of the month, your anniversary, your new officers, or an award you've received.

Q. Is it acceptable to invite a media celebrity to participate in a charitable event we're planning?

A. Yes. Most radio, TV, and print outlets allow their employees to appear on behalf of charitable foundations. If you can find a "connection," such as a member who knows the celebrity, you'll probably have better luck getting a positive response.

Q. How should I approach a columnist whom I'd like to see recommend my company's products?

A. Call the publication which runs the column and get the mailing address. Then start sending the columnist your press releases, along with cover letters commenting (positively) on recent columns. You might even send a media kit and suggest a timely topic for which you could be an interview source. Never demand coverage, though.

Q. Because my market niche is very narrow and my clientele is extremely limited, I'd like to know how to reach my potential customers without wasting time and money.

A. Aim your self-promotional efforts at "trade" publications only. Subscribe to industry-specific magazines to learn about conventions and other opportunities to speak to members. Join related associations, attend meetings regularly, and start sending your announcements to their newsletters.

Q. An article in the newspaper about my company contained numerous factual errors. Should I complain?

A. Unless the mistakes cast your business in a negative light you should probably forget about it, as the media is sensitive to criticism. If you do call the paper to request a correction, don't blame anyone — just ask for a published clarification. Or, you can write a letter to the editor which, when published, will correct any misstatements.

Q. My volunteer agency wants me to ask local newspapers to run our camera-ready display ad for free. Would this be good publicity?

A. An advertisement, whether you pay for its publication or not, is not publicity. Publicity refers to news stories and features such as press releases, calendar listings, and articles which are part of the "editorial" content of the print media. The added credibility of publicity comes from the perceived "third-party endorsement" of reporters and editors who have deemed you newsworthy enough for coverage.

Q. In the past seven years I've won numerous awards for my work and been interviewed by a number of national magazines, but I can't get my home town newspaper to mention my name. I've tried news releases, telephone calls, and even had friends write to the editor about me, but no luck. What can I do to get noticed?

A. It's time for a few fresh approaches. Try contributing a recipe to the food editor. Say "This is a quick pick-me-up I enjoy after working long hours at my desk." Open your home for a holiday house tour and send the decorating editor a personal invitation along with the press release. Volunteer to teach career skills at a prison and invite the news editor to send a photographer to your lecture.

Q. What's the best way to insure coverage of our most important annual event?

A. Contact your government's tourism agency and have the affair listed on the annual calendar of events. Many journalists and producers refer to these listings in order to find colorful stories for their publications and programs. Just be sure to place your request for a listing several months before the new year begins in order to meet the printer's deadline for the calendar.

Q. What's the best way to get on talk shows and demonstrate my amazing new invention?

A. Tie your query in with a seasonal theme or an appropriate observance by sending a press kit to producers with a cover letter pointing out the timeliness of your appearance. If your invention will aid boat owners, for instance, mention that during the summer people enjoy hearing about outdoor activities. If you've designed a new toy for pets, ask to be booked during National Pet Lovers Week. For a hair restorer, key your request to Father's Day.

Q. My business participates in quite a few charitable fundraisers such as fashion shows to help the homeless. Can we receive any media attention for such work?

A. Yes. Plan ahead for a memorable "photo op" by scheduling something visually exciting for a specific time, then sending a media advisory to all your local print and broadcast outlets. Just make sure there's convenient access to the scene when photographers and video crews arrive, with adequate space and electrical outlets for the cameras.

Q. My competition seems to get all the publicity while I receive none. How can I break into the local media?

A. Try going in a different direction from your competitors. If they're being featured in the business press for their profitability, you can capture the society section by becoming a patron of arts and co-sponsoring a black-tie musical event. If they're showing up on the evening television news, you can seek out a guest spot on the early morning radio talk shows.

Q. Is it possible to avoid negative press?

A. The best way to preserve a positive image in the media is to build a solid foundation with journalists, then maintain that good relationship. Begin by making sure the materials you send to the press are always properly prepared and free of factual errors. Then, take reporters' phone calls immediately, be honest, and speak in lively, quotable sound bites.

Q. During interviews I never seem to get my point across as clearly as I'd like. How can I improve my responses?

A. The first step in making the most of a media interview is knowing what you want to say. Here's an exercise to help you clarify your message: Write out several 15-second statements about your organization, your upcoming event, and whatever else you're publicizing. Rehearse and memorize them. Then work them smoothly into every interview you give by perfecting such verbal transitions as "Yes, John, and let me tell you what else we have planned..." or "We sure are, Mary, and another question I'm often asked is..."

Q. Is it worth the effort required to get publicity?

A. You bet it is! With her very first press kit mailing, a mushroom grower landed feature stories in three newspapers, filled several seminars to capacity, received a lucrative consulting contract from a university, and fielded offers from several publishers to write a book on mushroom growing. In another case, a brand-new nonprofit association spent less than $300 on materials and was featured in more than 100 articles and broadcasts, including cover stories in major magazines and member appearances on national television. Thanks to this publicity, in its first year the fledgling organization boasted new members in every corner of North America as well as England and Australia.

Even established individuals and groups can benefit, like the recreation association which discovered that getting media coverage was as simple as requesting it. "We never dreamed we were actually newsworthy," said the executive director, following several mentions in local newspapers. "And all these years, all we had to do was ask."